APPLIED TECHNIQUES IN
TRACK & FIELD

APPLIED TECHNIQUES IN
TRACK & FIELD

ED JACOBY

LEISURE PRESS

NEW YORK

A publication of
Leisure Press.
597 Fifth Avenue; New York, N.Y. 10017
Copyright © 1983 Leisure Press
All rights reserved. Printed in the U.S.A.

Library of Congress Catalog Card Number 82-81819

ISBN 0-88011-050-3

Cover design: Bobbi Sloan
Book design: Brian Groppe, Julie Garrison

Contents

Introduction

This book has been in the developmental stages for over ten years. My coaching experience is rapidly becoming a long term adventure! I have always been intrigued with the scientific aspects of physiology, psychology and bio-mechanics. Personal involvement in these sciences usually provides for sound skill development in applied track and field. And although I realize I am an amateur in these fields, over the years I have learned to use and apply as much technique to the skill development of the athlete as possible.

Having been a track coach for a long time, I am dedicated to coaching athletes and teaching physical education students as much about track and field as I know. You might say I have a "one track mind." I love it and my intention is that the student and athlete love it as well.

Basically, as I see it, coaching track and field requires a four-pronged approach. First and foremost, enthusiasm is the foundation. Enthusiasm more than anything makes up for mistakes of both the athlete and the coach. I would much rather see an enthusiastic athlete making mistakes than a highly skilled, drilled and *bored* person going through the motions of performance for some unknown reason. Give me an enthusiastic coach and I'll give you an enthusiastic athlete . . . give me an enthusiastic athlete, and I'll show you a winner who understands there are no limitations. Secondly, success in track and field coaching is preceded by sorting out and setting uncomplicated goals. Thirdly, once the goals have been established, the coach and athlete plan for reaching these objectives. The coach needs to set priorities in training, seasonal schedules and plans. These priorities must be directed toward reaching the pre-established goals. Lastly, organization is the key to effective track coaching. In most school programs, a coach with little or no additional help is responsible for ten to twenty events. Proper and careful preliminary planning is the only way a team-training session can be accomplished and do justice to all athletes.

It is the coach's responsibility to develop a meaningful training program for every athlete who takes the time and effort to participate. The true teacher works for the students, not themselves. When all is said and done, the evaluation of the teacher-coach is not what he or she taught the student or athlete to become; rather it is the student who says, "Look what I taught myself to become."

Acknowledgements

The author would like to acknowledge several individuals without whom the writing of this book would not have been possible.

John Tansley, the track coach at California State University at Long Beach, deserves much thanks and appreciation; he provided the photos and the permission to use the high speed film sequences contained throughout the book. These photos were originally owned and produced by the late Phil Bath, and are perhaps the best composite sequences ever produced in track and field.

My wife, Jean, who should be named co-author of this book, has put long and tireless hours of typing, editing and just being patient. She deserves much credit for the completion of the manuscript.

Two additional individuals helped tremendously in the preparation of individual chapters. Ray Lewis is the vault coach at Boise State University. His tireless efforts in working with pole vaulters of all ages throughout the Northwest have made him recognized as one of the best vault technicians around. Ray provided considerable advice, including a section on pole vault drills. Bill Bakley, a businessman by vocation and a coach by love, provided the entire chapter on the decathlon. Bill, a four-time All-American at Westmont College in California, coaches decathletes at Phoenix colleges and has in depth understanding of the event's complexities.

1

A Technical Guide to Distance Running: Introduction and Basic Information

The biggest concern of all interested distance coaches is to develop and direct a running program that will allow day-to-day success as well as provide the basis for progressive and complete development of an athlete's potential.

Many of us have worked with athletes who have developed seasonally meet-to-meet, and in some cases those athletes have surpassed our wildest expectations in competition and training. This may have been the result of careful planning and organization, or an understanding of physiological and psychological principles. Obviously, many coaches understand and apply these to a carefully planned program.

The problem is, however, that many coaches run a hit-or-miss program, in which one year they experience success and another, using similar methods with another group of athletes, show dismal results. The reason lies in the various levels of development, physical and psychological, of their athletes. The wise coach can fall back upon sound physiological advice and research for the stabilization of a training program.

A successful coach and runner must understand basic changes and characteristics that occur as the body responds to a variety of imposed stresses.

Until the 1960s, the American coach has little real understanding of research-related practices. Prior to this era our coaches were content to use what the Finns, Swedes, Germans and later the New Zealand athletes were using under the premise that if it was successsful for the foreign runner, it had to be successful for us, too. American coaches and runners used the smorgasbord approach; some quality athletes emerged, but many more young runners were driven away by discouragement and frustration than were able to develop satisfactorily.

Fortunately, there have been some pioneers in our coaching ranks who developed sound philosophies centering on our own society and using educationally based training goals.

Experience has shown it is impossible to coach effectively from a textbook. It is absolutely necessary for personalities to be taken into account. The personality of the coach and the personality of the athlete are equally important and the goals must be common. On one hand the athlete may expect the outcome of training to provide joy and serenity; the coach, on the other hand, expects to win meets for the high school or university. There must be a common tie and methods established to evaluate the "means." All attitudes and situations must be weighed carefully in program development.

Modern day attitudes concerning endurance training emerged largely through the efforts of the Finns and especially through the great Paavo Nurmi and his coach, Gosta Homer. Evolving at this time was a system of training labeled "Fartlek" (Speed Play). This eventually became the accepted mode of distance training on the international scene. Fartlek running differed from others as it combined an attitude of free expression with bursts of speed of varied distance and pace interspaced through a distance run. Most importantly, however, it initiated what we now understand to be uneven pace (slow and fast running). Regardless of the terminology attached to the various systems of endurance training, we now understand, through research and years of experience, that success in running depends upon the right proportions of long overdistance interspaced with some type of uneven pace training.

Even with the evolution of the Finnish training methods, there was little thought given to the reasons behind various kinds of training. The interest was, of course, in how much success the athletes experienced.

Soon after the Finnish techniques became well known, a similar type of program (alternating speeds) emerged from another European country— Germany. This program slowly began to overshadow all other methods of endurance training.

It is now well understood that an organism cannot develop unless it undergoes a period of overload training. Overload must occur in one or all of the following situations:
● Increase the speed of performance.
● Increase the total load.
● Increase the total time a position or activity is performed.
● Increase the total number of performances.

Different work loads effect the body differently. It is said if you wish to increase strength and endurance you need to increase the threshold of stress by one-third the normal activity. Depending upon the goal, different functions and body areas respond to varied overload percentages. The spleen shows development with 20% of maximum work levels, the heart responds to approximately 35%, the adrenal gland responds to 70%, and the neuromuscular speed mechanism responds to 85-100% work loads.

This leads to a very important consideration: how much is enough and how much is too much?

Hans Selye's theories have great meaning to coaches and athletes. According to Selye, there is only so much adaptation that can take place in training. When the response hormones are depleted, they do not (in short periods of time,) replenish themselves. When they are depleted, we see staleness, fatigue and injury in athletes. This basically is what Selye refers to as the General Adaptation Syndrome (GAS).

Ideally, development through training occurs gradually by means of small stressors. As the athlete or bodily system meets and accepts these stresses he or she not only makes an adequate adjustment but over-compensates. The response will be somewhat greater than simply meeting the stress at hand.

This pattern of growth and development, as long as the stress is within the range of a rather easy response, is called training. When the stress is not within the range of easy response, it is called straining. The principle works like an individual muscle. When overload is applied at a moderate rate, strength will increase. But if you are greedy and attempt to do the impossible, strain and physical or emotional injury can occur.

Basically, stress in moderate amounts will enhance development. However, not only are physical stressors involved, we further complicate the total process with personalities, personal problems, etc. and force situations that cause strain rather than physical advancement.

Let's take the case of a distance runner. Physical training for distance running will not, under ordinary circumstances, create a demand on the total body. A runner's training most often is concerned with meeting physical demands. Unfortunately, most coaches assume that physical development is the only important item. Therefore, the physically-prepared athlete goes into competition and immediately encounters new emotional stresses (fear of competition, fear of defeat, fear of failure or even fear of success). Alone or in combination any of these emotions can drain the nervous energies before competition begins.

Anxiety results from stress. In fact, anxiety and stress are somewhat related. Simply speaking, the difference between stress and anxiety lies in the fact that stress can be handled and anxiety either is not handled or at least for the time being is tabled. Anxiety is a pent up feeling of frustration that seemingly is beyond our control.

If stress can be a learning situation, or a motivator, then it will inspire the athlete. However, if stress leads to frustration beyond control, then it creates anxiety and over a period of time will ultimately lead to strain and injury.

The human organism needs a support triangle—one side is physical, one side is emotional and one side is social. If any side lacks strength, the total structure will crumble.

Stress anywhere on this supporting structure affects the physiological function of the athlete. Stress imposed on an individual is met by body changes that include:

- Increased blood sugar
- Increased adrenal secretion
- Parasympathetic shutdown
- Blood coagulation

Luckily, most anxieties in athletes can be neutralized by physical activity, which either does away with or minimizes the prior characteristics. This is why most athletes do not develop ulcers or heart and circulation problems with the same frequency as the general population who cope with similar anxiety problems but usually have no physical release. Athletes, on the other hand, may respond to anxiety by general staleness and/or contempt for their program, coach or teammates.

Overload stress placed upon the body is specific in nature. The body will adapt to stress placed upon those areas for which it is trained. But it must be remembered that one specific stress placed upon an athlete will not greatly influence the body against other specific stresses, such as emotional stress.

Specificity of training is a must to allow an athlete's progressive development. Slow training naturally will not produce a fast athlete; neither will training on flat terrain produce an effective hill runner. But both are necessary, as is further specific training for those other specific areas.

General objectives must be selected according to the basic needs of the athlete, then specific training plans must be related to the task at hand. General goal selection in training should include the following questions:

- What areas of the body (physiological and psychological) need to be improved for an athlete to become effective in the particular event?
- What type of training work is effective to the above areas of the body?
- What is suitable in terms of frequency and duration of the varied training techniques? Must a base of work preclude sharpening work?
- What are the determining factors that produce a training effect as opposed to a straining effect?

Objectives When Setting Up A Running Program

When developing any endurance running program, the question needs to be asked, "What are we preparing to accomplish?" Initially a runner needs to develop an endurance base, which is done specifically through cardio-vascular training. We move up the ladder gradually into more specific responses including: muscular endurance, pace judgement and power running on the hills (this includes the mechanics of running). Finally, in the later stages of our program plan, we include repetition running for the development of speed and strength. These are all obvious physiological ingredients of distance programming but do not include emotional or psychological aspects.

Types of endurance training and their general progression include over-distance, interval training, repetition training, sprint and power or weight training. Weight training is included at the later stages of the listed progressions because it is so important in speed work. Inversely, speed training does a great deal for strength work.

The physiological effects of specific training include the following characteristics:

1. **Overdistance**
   A. Increases steady state
   B. Increases capillary count in working muscle
   C. Increases oxygen uptake
   D. Increases the capacity of the veins and arteries to carry blood
   E. Increases aerobic processes
2. **Interval Training**
   A. Increases the size and strength of the heart
   B. Increases the stroke volume of the heart
   C. Increases the oxygen pulse
   D. Promotes some anaerobic characteristics
3. **Repetition Training**
   A. Increases anaerobic characteristics
   B. Increases ability to buffer waste materials
   C. Increases speed and strength characteristics
4. **Spring Training**
   A. Increases the number of active muscle fibers
   B. Thickens and toughens the sarcolemma of muscle fiber and increases the amount of connective tissue within the muscle
   C. Increases the strength and development of power
   D. Increases speed and coordination
   E. Increases muscle size especially in the white muscle fibers
5. **Weight and Power Training**
   A. Increase of myofibrils

An increased vital capacity of the lungs is characteristic of overload training.

B. Thickening of the sarcolemma and connective tissue
C. Capillary development

Physiological Characteristics of Endurance Training

Realistically, there are four main areas of concern in endurance training. Listed in order of progressive use, they are:
(1) general or total body endurance,
(2) heart endurance,
(3) local muscle endurance, and
(4) motor unit efficiency.

In developing a model program, we must bring the components together in a commonsense manner, moving from a foundation of overall strength and endurance to neural pattern development as expressed by the stimulus response aspects of learning.

Endurance training lies in developing the following physiological goals:

- The vital capacity of the lungs and the permeability of the pulmonary membrane.
- The stroke volume of the heart per minute.
- Autoregulation of local capillaries.
- The buffering capacity of the bicarbonate ions in the circulation and the working muscles.
- Increased capillary count in active muscles (capillarization).
- The amount of oxygen and carbon dioxide carrying hemoglobin and the number of red blood cells.
- The amount of phosphocreatine and adenosine triphosphate stored in the muscles and blood.
- Hormone secretions of the pituitary, gonads and adrenal glands.

In analyzing the above list, we see some characteristics of strength development added to the necessary requirements for simple endurance training; however, it is assumed for conditioning that it is impossible to have endurance without certain aspects of strength development following naturally.

Increased vital capacity of the lungs is characteristic of overload training. This implies lung adaptation through increased vital holding ability. It is brought about by increased volume pressure which must be classed as an over compensation. As the lung volume increases, the membrane surrounding the inside surfaces of the lungs is exposed to greater surface area, thus providing a greater capacity for gaseous exchange. It is felt by some (but not definitely known) that increase in lung size causes the membrane to become thinner, increasing the gas

17

transport across the pulmonary membrane.

The heart varies in size and weight through training. In endurance activity there is a slight size increase. This is partially due to hypertrophy, but the primary heart size increase occurs through dilation, as expressed by increased holding capacity. Thus the organ is able to hold more and put out more blood during the same time interval as the heart of the nontrained individual.

We also conclude that overload increases systolic stroke force, and the mean contraction time is greatly reduced through training. Efficiency is, therefore, attributed to greater inside volume and a stronger and quicker contractile force.

Autoregulation, which is the ability of the circulatory system to carry more blood, is characterized in the athlete in two major ways. The short term variety is expressed in the untrained, as well as in the trained individual. The active muscles readily deplete the oxygen content in the surrounding blood and, consequently, a high concentration of carbon dioxide is present. Sensory receptors stimulate an automatic nerve process which immediately dilates the arterioles in the area, thus allowing greater blood flow. The long term autoregulation is basically a continuation of the above. Again, there is the automatic stimulation of the chemoreceptors and the reflex of dilation; however, the capillaries will remain dilated, even when the athlete is not training.

Bufferization of the hydrogen heavy waste materials produced during muscle activity is of the utmost importance in reducing fatigue and allowing continued activity over a prolonged period of time. In summary, bufferization is the ability of the bicarbonate ion to combine with strong acids and convert them into weak acids which later can be split into water and allow carbon dioxide to be removed from the body through urine and expiration.

Capillarization is characteristic of a greatly increased number of capillaries surrounding an area that is subjected to repetitions of continuous contractions and overload. It has been said that through high repetitions the capillary count can increase upward from forty to fifty percent.

Hemoglobin concentration is important to all endurance activities. It has the unique capacity to combine with oxygen and carbon dioxide, thus serving the dual function of removing waste and supplying needed oxidation to the cell. The hemoglobin count shows increases that are directly proportional to the red blood cell increases. This is accomplished through the erythropoietic stimulation of the bone marrow.

Phosphocreatine is the material necessary for immediate muscular contractions. When the present supply of this material is used, the body goes into oxygen debt until adenosine diphosphate (ADP) is resynthesized to adenosine triphosphate (ATP), used to reconvert waste to energy.

In discussing hormones in relation to the efficiency of intensity training, we must first consider those hormones concerned with growth development. These are normally produced in the pituitary gland and have to do with protein synthesis, carbohydrate metabolism, and general growth characteristics. Hormone secretion is not unique for those undergoing training programs. However, local stress needs designate "extra secretions." Additional needs stem from adaptation to stress in various forms. The sex glands give additional impetus through secretions of testosterone which especially effects strength development and tends to yield increases in muscle mass. The primary hormone of special concern (which is influenced by repetition and interval training and will be discussed later in more detail) is that coming from the suprarenal gland. Prokop and Selye speak of the adaptation hormone—specifically, the hormones secreted from the adrenal cortex and the suprarenal glands. These glands react to stress as applied to body adaptation. This is of critical importance as a depletion of this material is characterized by an immediate drop-off in training and competition performance.

Although the exact mechanisms of the adrenal glands reaction to stress is not known at this time, it is definitely understood that through the adrenal cortex, there is the ability to develop adaptation of bodily processes to applied stimuli. It has been shown that during activity there is increased hydrocortisone and aldosterone (secretions of the cortex of the adrenal gland). Early investigations suggest that any increase in the size of the adrenal glands would have a direct correlation to the amount of secretions. Later studies, however, indicate that size increase had little correlation to the amount secreted. Glandular hypertrophy begins with increased training loads approximately one to three weeks after beginning activity, and then an additional increase in approximately the sixth week of training. The secretions of this gland increase according to the size increase up to the third week; after that the secretions and size begin to level off and, in some cases, decrease during the latter phase of the hypertrophy.

Through a review of certain aspects of the known metabolic functions of the adrenal cortical hormones, we can generalize about the adaptation of an athlete's body when training. Basically, the coach is concerned with the electrolyte concentration and fluid balance within the body.

The electrolyte balance is regulated by aldosterone which is secreted by the adrenal cortex. The positive and negative ion concentration relating to fluid control is expressed by the following:

- Control of excessive loss of sodium and water from the kidneys, sweat glands, and gastrointestinal tract.
- The ability to retain potassium.
- The control of acceptable levels of acid concentration.
- The ability to decrease and increase plasma and extracellular fluids.

● To decrease or increase the diuretic release of fluid volume.

Aldosterone secretions can be increased by several stimuli; but of special importance in this discussion are circumstances which cause a decrease in plasma and extracellular fluid volumes. Such situations are usually characterized by extreme body temperatures brought about by physical exertion and low body fluids. As the aldosterone level increases, there is noticeable increase of plasma and extracellular fluid, thus more efficient balance of the potassium and sodium necessary for nerve impulse transmission.

Two additional hormones, androgen and glucocorticoid, are also of great importance to the athlete's ability to increase his/her work load. The hormones work in counter activity, one having anabolic and the other catabolic characteristics. Basically, this consists of protein fabrication via the androgens and protein metabolism through the glucocorticoids.

The main function of the androgens, secreted by either the cortex of the adrenal glands or by the sex glands, is protein anabolism. Specifically, this makes possible the build up and storage of protein in the body. It has been established that injections or supplementary administrations of androgens (anabolic steroids) show increased "fabrication" of structural protein and decreased body fat. The changes that occurred were most prominent in the muscles, sex glands and sex accessory organs, and, to a lesser extent, in the liver and the kidneys.

The basic function of androgen secretion is protein "fabrication"—the specific bodily activity that creates a positive nitrogen (component of protein) balance through retaining this compound in the body. In addition phosphorous, sodium, potassium and sulfur are also necessary for protein synthesis and are, therefore, retained in the body fluids. The retention of the previously discussed materials is a direct result of the aldosterone secretions from the adrenal cortex.

The other important adrenal cortex secretion is glucocorticoid. Glucocorticoids effect blood and liver glucose homeostasis (normal or stable levels of an organism). Homeostasis is accomplished through carbohydrate and protein metabolism. Glucocorticoids basically function to stimulate the conversion of proteins to carbohydrates. The presence of glucocorticoids is shown by the additional nitrogen concentration in the urine of the athlete. This same phenomena leads physiologists to believe that glucocorticoids may serve the additional function of gluconeogenesis (converting fats to usable carbohydrates). This is a major source of energy for the distance runner.

In addition to the above functions, there is further evidence that cortico-secretions alter the functional ability of striated muscle. The absence of corticosteroids allows the muscle to become weak and easily fatigued, although the exact reason for this is unknown. Interestingly, large doses of hydrocortisones, a glucocorticoid, over long periods of time, produce muscle wasting by increasing energy producing materials from structural protein. The same is true when cortisones are injected into injury sites over long periods of time.

The heart and the circulatory system also show interdependence upon adrenocortical activity. First, there is a feed back effect from the electrolyte balance which is explained as gauged by aldosterone. Too little aldosterone causes a decreased amount of potassium, and too much can cause myocardial arrest.

Further, and perhaps the most important, action of the adrenal secretions lie in the oxidative capacity of a training athlete. Increased activity stimulates the cortex of the adrenal gland, thus in turn increasing the size and number of the mitochondria of the tissue and muscle cell.

It has been found that mitochondria are especially important to us in any working activity. They hold the potential of oxidizing carbohydrates into carbon dioxide and water while yielding the high energy compound of adenosine triphosphate (ATP), the basic component for energy. The more mitochondria present, the more energy is liberated, and the more total work is expected.

In program development centered around physiological characteristics of training, the coach and athlete must be aware of generalized attitudes. In most cases it is impractical or even impossible to train specific body systems independently. The human organism does not operate as a group of separate entities, rather it functions as a physical, emotional and social whole.

However, it is necessary to understand the physiological response to be expected from a specific mode of training. Much consideration should be given to the either physiological areas listed in the beginning of the chapter. These progressions should serve as targets leading to individualized training programs. Through a good understanding of basic physiology, a coach can program both specifically and generally.

After gaining some insight into the foregoing analysis of adaptations and body changes, select questions should begin to emerge. Specifically, the coach wishes to learn the physiological effects of the more common and accepted training methods. What types of training should be applied and for what reason? Figure 1-1 is a simple but explicit summary of what types of training precipitate specific physiological processes.

Spindler, John. "The Physiological Basis of Interval Training, Part One," UNITED STATES TRACK COACHES ASSOCIATION QUARTERLY REVIEW, December, 1966.

Proper weight training can improve both strength and speed.

FIGURE 1-1

PHYSIOLOGICAL EFFECT ON MUSCULATURE CARDIO-VASCULAR SYSTEM				
Means of Training	Coordination and Strength	Metabolism	Heart	Capillaries
1. Weight training, body building circuit method.	MAXIMAL hypertrophy; gain in strength, speed; sarcolemma thickens.	Increase in alkaline reserve with circuit method; energy storage.	Is not increased; no effect.	MINIMAL Capillarization.
2. Sprints.	MAXIMAL increase in speed and coordination; motor units efficiency increased; development of power.	Small increase in alkaline reserve.	MINIMAL increase in heart size; no effect.	Capillarization small.
3. Fast-tempo runs	Less increase in speed, less hypertrophy of muscles.	MAXIMAL increase in alkaline reserve; bufferization; increased capacity for oxygen debt; energy storage.	Relatively small increase in heart size; no effect.	Stronger capillarization.
4. Interval running.	No increase in speed, no hypertrophy of muscles.	Energy storage.	MAXIMAL increase in stroke volume. MAXIMAL increase in oxygen pulse.	Considerably stronger capillarization; increased oxygen intake.
5. Long distance runs.	MINIMAL hypertrophy; no gain in strength; decrease in muscle size for marathon.	Energy storage; higher efficiency done in steady state; higher economization.	Less increase in the stroke volume as in 4; ratio stroke volume/weight of body high.	MAXIMAL capillarization and oxygen intake.

Training Methods And Sequential Arrangements As Applied To Physiology

1. Overdistance Training

During the early season, especially the off season, it is extremely important to use running overdistance as a preparation base for later training and competitive efforts. In fact, before launching into any moderate to heavy training, the athlete must prepare themself with a minimum of 10-12 weeks of steady, long distance running.

The coach and athlete must understand that at the onset of training the athlete's blood volume increases up to twenty percent. That is, if the usual volume is five liters, then, through training over a period if time, the volume would rise to six liters. Due to this, the blood tends to be diluted as the hemoglobin and red blood cell production do not progress hand-in-hand with the increased blood volume. At this time the athlete is very susceptible to fatigue, injury and illness.

Basic blood dilution is the only stimulus that excites the production of red blood cells by the bone marrow through exercise.

It takes three to four weeks for the equilibrium between blood volume and red blood cell concentration to occur; therefore, a drop in red blood cell concentration should be considered natural in a training program. In addition, the phenomena serves as a direct indicater; if the red blood cell count drops below the ten percent level, the training program has been too severe. During blood analysis, consideration should also be given to the eosinophil count; a big drop in the concentration of this white blood cell indicates a too severe training program. Also, if the concentraiton is well over the normal amount, it is an indication of infection. During the three to four-week time necessary to reach blood cell plasma equilibrium, steady overdistance work should be the primary means of training. Any training more severe could cause physical and emotional problems to the athlete in a progressive program.

Overdistance training is explained as a slow pace for a progressively increasing number of miles. The assumption is: early work pointed aimed at general overall development provides a foundation for the severe training in later phases. Judging from the nature of this type of running, the coach could expect the following: (1) The runner receives the full benefits of capillarization from maximum constant repetitions of movement. Additional benefits are received through autoregulation of the short term, and over a period of ten to fourteen days, permanent dilation of the arterioles would be initiated. (2) Little or no hypertrophy of muscles. In fact, observation shows that marathon training frequently reduces muscle mass. (3) Also phosphocreatine or energy storage will occur in varied levels while training at the steady state.

2. Interval Training

After a period of two to two and one-half weeks of overdistance work, we progress to the second phase of our program. This includes the use of a moderate interval type program. Here the athlete is to perform pace intervals of a desired length (usually from 100 to 400 meters) from thirty to fifty percent of maximal ability, and with a resting (jogging seems to give best results) recovery that has a duration of less than total recovery. Pulse return can be designated by experimentation. Assume that the mean heart rate is 180 beats/minute at the end of the working interval; we now have to determine the amount of time required for the mean pulse rate to descend to 120 beats/minute.

The physiological basis of the interval method is based on the premise that the stimuli for the regulative dilation of the heart are provided primarily by demands on the stroke volume and not so much by demands on the blood pressure.

Cardiac development actually takes place during the resting phase of interval training. At this time there is increased oxygen uptake and a lower median arterial blood pressure. Studies show that increased beat volumes (stroke volumes) during the recovery period are the stimuli for the increase in heart size and performance. This dilation and hypertrophy is an inescapable condition for the increase of heart capacity and heart strength during interval training.

It is generally agreed by physiologists that the resting interval not only gives a period of physiological recovery but also points to cardiac dilation, which in turn is necessary for overload adaptation. This is, of course, the basic point of stress adaptation in repetition training of moderate intensity and especially in the true interval training.

After an interval of work, there is an immediate elevation in oxygen consumption. We find the greatest incidence of this oxygen consumption occurs during the first half minute following the performance. The depth of external respiration does not become greater, but the respiratory rate does increase during the exertion.

The second very important consideration shows the mean arterial pressure increases during the interval of work with a significant decrease during the resting pause. Furthermore, the pulse rate shows no increase even though an elevation in oxygen intake is occurring.

For this reason the "oxygen pulse" is the highest during the first half of the recovery period. Experiments seem to imply this high "oxygen pulse" is indicative of economical oxygen transportation. Spindler's point-by-point summary of Dr. Reindell's test conclusions suggest the following:

● The increased oxygen intake in the beginning of the recovery pause is an indication there are also heavy demands on the organism during the recovery pause.

- The performance is accomplished with a relatively low pulse and low blood pressure.
- Since the arterio-venous difference is not great immediately after the performance, the increased oxygen transport is only made possible by a greater stroke volume.
- The increase in the stroke volume of the recovery pause (phase) is the most efficient stimulus for the relative, adaptive dilation of the heart.
- The volume demand is the effective stimulus for the regulative dilation of the heart.
- The main stimulus for the adaptation process does not occur during the single performance but during the recovery phase. To attain the optimum intensity of the stimuli, the recovery phase should not be too long. With a longer recovery, the shifting of blood in the circulatory system prevents the ideal conditions for the optimum stroke volume increase. Another reason a shorter recovery phase is that the capillaries do not allow the same flow 3 or 4 minutes after the performance.
- The intensity must be chosen so that during the performance and the recovery the conditions exist for optimum stimulus of all four chambers of the heart.

Through large scale experimentation, which included three thousand separate investigations, the Gerschler-Reindell Law was developed in respect to principles governing the application of interval training. This law is that, during the course of exercise, the heart does not exceed one hundred eighty beats per minute. Therefore, evidently, one hundred eighty beats represents a limit under moderate or sub intensity performances. It has been reported by Counsilman that, in his pulse records of swimmers, a rate of two hundred would not be uncommon while participating in repetition work. However, it should be pointed out that these were speed conditions of seventy percent or above intensities, and, of course, as explained below, he uses a near full recovery before going to the next interval.

Inserting the interval law toward a working model, Gerschler allowed a maximum of one minute and thirty seconds to return to the ideal 120-125 beats/minute and then immediately repeated the next working interval. If this recovery is not completed in the one minute and thirty second rest interval, then it must be assumed that the work demand was either too extreme, or the duration of effect was too long.

3. Repetition (Fast Tempo Running)

Our third consideration in the progression of the training program is repetition or fast tempo running.

Interval training for local muscle endurance, as expressed by Gerschler, is in reality what Americans more commonly call "repetition running" or "fast tempo running." In effect the German terminology includes moderate interval work and speed interval work.

In attempting to differentiate terminology of interval training and repetition training, consider that repetition training is concerned with a type of program in which near maximum intensity (seventy percent or more) is performed. The unique aspect here is that near total recovery periods are prescribed in order that the pulse rate return to under 120 beats/minute. This means a recovery period from four to six minutes, and upwards of eight to ten minutes.

This specific technique relates principally to local muscle endurance. Local muscle endurance is characteristically important to interval and repetition training but is somewhat neglected in other means of training.

"Physiologically, local muscle endurance equals the ability of cells to adjust to a state of oxygen debt ... In practice, local muscle endurance equals the ability of the muscles to absorb and maintain intensive strain from the fast motion movement sequences." (Gerschler)

This added efficiency through training comes about only with practice of high repetitions through a moderately fast rate of speed carried through a short time duration.

Repetition training is expressed by intensity levels of seventy percent effort or above for a given distance and by a near complete resting recovery period. Instead of waiting for the pulse to return to near 120, we wish the recovery to descend to approximately 100 or below. Full recovery training shows the following effect:

- Neurologically, there is a definite increase in speed and coordination, but again, this development is directly related to the speed or effort. If the intensity level is nearer to ninety or one hundred percent, the motor unit efficiency will be higher than if the intensity load is near seventy percent.
- Intramuscular evaluation would show maximal alkaline reserve (additional) amounts available. This material is necessary for efficient acid bufferization. The phenomena is developed because the athlete immediately goes into oxygen debt, and does not allow sufficient time for reconversion of some of the lactic acid into glycogen. Following the recovery, the athlete immediately goes back into oxygen debt utilizing the available phosphocreatine. Therefore, in fast tempo running there is an over compensation by the adaptation hormone reflecting local areas in trying to supply enough alkaline for bufferization during the need period.

4. Sprint Or Speed Training

The final phase of our overall plan is speed training. This is typically 90-100 percent effort or intensity. Again, the athlete goes full speed for a

When over-stimulations occur, the only alternative in training is a decrease in workload or rest.

predetermined distance, then waits until near full recovery before performing the next phase of the workout. The primary consideration is a direct increase of running speed, so most development is in neuronal and motor unit efficiency. Speed running shows increases in hypertrophy of skeletal muscles, particularly in the white muscle fibers, as well as coordination and power. However, there is no noticeable increase in heart size and minimal increase in capillarization.

Relating to neuromuscular development, efficiency is demonstrated by agility, increased stride pattern, and increased joint flexibility. Additional adaptations occur through neuronal facilitation in he central nervous system. There are particular adaptations in the cerebellum such as predictability of exact positioning of all movement patterns which lead to stride length and body angle during running.

Glandular Adaptation To Endurance Training

Prokop and Selye write of certain aspects of adrenal gland functioning as related to overload training. Their investigations show there is a direct increase in size and secretions of the suprarenal hormones which are now assumed to be the adaptation regulators. In applying increased interval training loads (that of running and swimming on experimental hamsters), significant increases were shown in the mass of the heart and the adrenal gland, and especially the cortex.

Experimental animals were divided into groups representing a percentage of maximal work load applied—eighteen percent, thirty-six percent, seventy percent and one hundred percent. These animals were then compared to a control group which underwent no training program. The comparison showed an increase in size and weight of the adrenal up to the seventy percent group. A maximum heart hypertrophy was shown up to the thirty-six percent training level but with no increase beyond this in any of the other three intensity level groups, thus indicating a moderate intensity of activity of thirty-six percent provides all the cardiac development possible. Experiments also suggested that additional loads did not increase heart size.

In summarization, we can reach conclusions on the following. Moderate work loads, at a certain distance (thirty to forty percent of maximum at this distance with a short recovery of rest), will give maximal cardiac development. However, when wishing to increase the adaptability of prolonged stress, we tend to point the athlete toward faster repetitions—for example, seventy percent of maximum speed for that particular distance. In addition, the higher levels of intensity, seventy to ninety percent of maximal, also show improvement of coordination and local muscle development.

Secondary considerations show that experimental animals in high intensity programs (seventy percent or above) reacted to stress for a period of time, then began to retrogress and show symptoms of fatigue. It was demonstrated that over-stimulation of the suprarenal gland caused a depletion of adaptation hormones and consequently the ability to adapt to stress was lost.

This clearly indicates that one cannot expect a one hundred percent peak in performance or training over an extended period of time. When over-stimulations occur, the only alternative in training is a decrease in work load or a rest.

Presently, work is being conducted on the practicability of urinalysis in determining the operational level of suprarenal secretion. The amount of kilosteroids in the urine normally shows a certain relationship. If the level of this material rises, it is felt by some researchers to be an indication of overstimulation of the suprarenal glands and that the training intensity is too great.

Figures 1-2 and 1-3 show Prokop's correlation of organic development as compared to percentage of intensity level training. It should be noted however, that this comes from animal experimentation.

From these investigations, we assume that there is a comparable ratio to secretions and the size of the gland. By training at 70% of maximum, the athlete receives full benefits of the adrenal gland. Also when training at 36%, the athlete receives the necessary stimuli for heart development. Training at higher levels will not cause further development of either of these glands.

Sample Distance—Middle Distance

Progression Program

This program, adapted from a variety of other successful programs, has proven itself over several years. It is initiated when the athletes arrive on campus and a determination is made to see if they are in good condition. This is measured by the athlete's ability to run at a six minute pace for 8-10 miles. This level of fitness is necessary to permit a runner to participate in our organized program.

There is a separate program for cross country and track. Date pace in cross country is arbitrarily set to enhance general physiological progressions and to adapt runners to effective team running as is necessary in cross country. Date pace in track is established individually by running a trial distance at approximately ¾ effort.

Goal pace is established through close analysis by the coach and athlete. Consideration is given to last season's experience in racing situations, strength, competitive racing ability, etc.

FIGURE 1-2

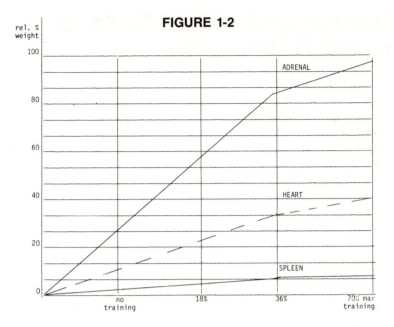

FIGURE 1-3
Sample Workload Progression for an Athlete Who Has Maximum Speed of Approximately 22.8 200 Meter Speed

percent of workload	Work load equals the percent of maximum ability	
	Rest interval equals the mean time required for the pulse to return to 140 (in intervals) or 100 (in repetitions).	
Moderate Interval 36% of maximum	WORK LOAD INTERVAL	37.7 seconds
	REST (JOGGING)	approximately 30.0 seconds
Fast Interval 60% of maximum	WORK LOAD INTERVAL	32.2 seconds
	REST (JOGGING)	approximately 40.0 seconds
Moderate repetitions 80% of maximum	WORK LOAD REPETITION 27.6 seconds	
	REST (JOGGING) FULL RECOVERY 4-8 minutes	
Sprint repetitions	WORK LOAD REPETITION 23.0 seconds	
	REST (JOGGING) FULL RECOVERY 4-8 minutes	

Distance And Middle Distance Runner Training Outline

Summer Training

New runners, or runners who consider themselves in poor physical condition, begin with an easy 30 minute run for the first two or three sessions. This should be an away run, one which is done at a speed comfortable to the runner. Pick a suitable and interesting course and run away from the central spot for fifteen minutes, then return. Each successive time out, you should increase the time away by two to four minutes. Again, the pace must be comfortable.

All running in the summer should be done for fitness and recreation. Never allow your summer runs to turn into a stress situation. "Do as you feel."

August— Transition to team running

Prior to the time we train as a team, the athlete should make some preparations toward being capable of handling group workouts when he arrives on campus. He is *not* ready to train until he can perform a run with no undue stress for a period of one and one-half hours. At this time *only* do we begin a varied pace progression workout.

Monday— 10 X miles in hills or rolling cross country course at ½ effort.

Tuesday— 12 X miles flat area at ¼ effort.

Wednesday— 6 X miles of fartlek running (I will provide the necessary information for this type of running).

Thursday— 12 X miles flat area at ¼ effort.

Friday— 10 X miles over original course at faster than original time.

Saturday— 14 X miles at ¼ effort (flat running).

Sunday— Run of your choice.

Total mileage—approximately 70 miles.

Two weeks before reporting to practice, the athlete should follow this general plan. The second week is essentially the same as the first with the exception that the runner should include alternate days of hill running. They will be tested upon their arrival on campus with our annual 8 or 10 mile test run. This is performed the Saturday morning prior to the start of school. Our course tests condition with its variety of terrain. It includes several long hills.

September— Transitional period

During our early training sessions, we undertake a program consisting of (1) over-distance, (2) fartlek, (3) varied distance and pace running. In addition, each athlete is required to meet, with the group for a morning run at approximately 7:00 a.m. All morning running is for easy distance from 3-6 X miles.

Cross Country General Training Plan For Weeks During Non-Competitive Season

Monday— Distance, varied pace on hills
Tuesday— Repeat miles or 1320's
Wednesday— Long distance at steady pace
Thursday— Pace 440's
Friday— Medium distance run
Saturday— a.m. hard start 1320 (increasing pace 440), example (65-75-85) equals 3:45—then steady running for 4 miles, 1320 (steady pace) race training pace, example (70-70-70) equals 4:00—then steady running for 4 more miles—then 1320 with decreasing pace 440, example (80-70-65)
Sunday— Easy 12-15

Cross Country General Training Plan For Weeks During Competitive Season

Monday— Distance, varied pace, finish with decreasing pace 110's or 165's
Tuesday— Repeat pace running 880, 1320 or miles. Finish with 220-330-440 drop downs
Wednesday— Steady distance running
Thursday— Pace 440's—Follow with drop down set
Friday— Warm-up
Saturday— Compete
Sunday— Easy 12-15 mile run

Key to progression pace other than standard 440 yard as cited—for date pace times through November 28. (Team training priority)

110 yards	1.5 to 2.5 slower than best 110
220 yards	3.0 to 5.0 slower than best 220
440 yards	0 to 4.0 slower or faster than standard (date pace)
880 yards	4 secs slower per 440 than standard (date pace)
Mile	4 secs slower per 440 than standard (date pace)

Interval, Month, Week Pace Chart With Volume and Interval Period

All the training performed during the coming year will be done in a sequence that should be gradual enough for all runners, yet can be of such quantity and quality that will tax the best of them. THE MAIN CONCERN IS THAT THE ATHLETE PROGRESS WITH THE SCHEDULE, AND NEVER TRY TO GET AHEAD OF THE PROGRESSION (Fig. 1-4).

It is now known that staleness, if we wish to call it that, is not from doing too much—it's from trying to do too much too soon.

FIGURE 1-4

Sequence	Week	Date Train Pace	Mileage As To Race Distance	Recovery Interval Jog	Team Monthly Goal Pace For Sets (Training Only)
Cycle #1	1	76	2 x	full-½	440-Drop down & at will
	2	76	2-4 x	½	880-2:16 (33)
	3	76	2-4 x	½	Mile-4:40 (70)
	1	76	3-8 x	¼	3 Mile-15:00 (5:00)
Cycle #2	2	74	3 x	full	440-Drop down — at will
	3	74	3-4 x	½	880-(2:10) (32)
	1	74	3-4 x	¼	Mile-(4:32) (68)
	2	74	3-4 x	¼	3 Mile-14:40 (4:56)
Cycle #3	3	72	4-5 x	full	880-2:05 (31)
	1	72	3-4 x	½	Mile-4:20 (65)
					3 Mile-14:20 (4:50)
Cycle #4	2				Begin Individualization
	3				long, easy runs
Cycle #5	1				light intervals
	2				3/4 effort trials
	3	Christmas			mileage 85-100 mi./week
	1	Vacation			Run at home-maintain
Cycle #6	2				mileage.
	3				
	1				long runs
	2				Hill intervals, light interval
Cycle #7	3				Indoor meets for test efforts
	1				
	2				
	3				Oregon system
Cycle #8	1				Hard, easy
	2				Date pace, Goal pace
	3				
	1				
Cycle #9	2				
	3				
	1				
	2				
Cycle #10	3				
	1				
	2				Taper & speed
	3				

Distance And Middle Distance Runners' Cycle Program For Spring Track Season

Upon evaluating the foregoing progressive monthly program for distance and middle distance runners, an attempt is made to group all runners into a basic program until cross country is over. At this time, runners should be "individualized" according to event abilities and goals. For this reason it is advantageous to develop a cycle program to help meet the individual needs of the athletes. (Fig. 1-5).

FIGURE 1-5

SAMPLE CYCLE PROGRAM FOR TRACK SEASON

Meeting Times Sunday:

Conley	7:00 p.m.	Knapp	9:00 p.m.
Steffens	7:30 p.m.	Stewart	(Monday morning)
Blackburn	8:00 p.m.	Birt	— — — —
Rothenberger	8:30 p.m.	Cable	— — — —

December 11 - January 20	Overdistance Goal 120 miles
January 20-March 1	Powertraining (Hill Emphasis)
March 1-April 15	Date Pace - Goal Pace
April 15-June 1	Speed - Goal (Hard-Easy-Easy)

OVERDISTANCE (appx. 40 days)

1. #1 Fartlek (Lydiard) (No sequence)
2. Long Sustained 1/2 - 3/4 effort
3. #2 Fartlek (Homer) Quality
4. Hills
5. Test Runs
6. Long Intervals

POWERTRAINING (appx. 40 days)

1. Hill Intervals (No more than once each 14 days)
2. Hill Circuit (Fartlek Base)
3. Lydiard Fartlek
4. Long Runs
5. Short Hill Repeats & Hill Hops or Stadium

DATE PACE - GOAL PACE (appx. 45 days)

1. Fartlek - Homer (3 x 14 day sequences)
2. Repetitions Pace Long Recovery
3. Sets of Intervals & Ladders
4. Short Hills or Stadium Stairs

SPEED & SPEED MAINTAINENCE (appx. 45 days)

1. Goal Pace & Faster (no sequence to be set around competition)

In December we like to begin on cycles with an emphasis on large volumes of work. In June our individual work ends in competition with conference and national meets.

Perhaps the most important aspect of this cycle is the individual counseling between coach and athlete. In these weekly sessions, discussions center on weekly and seasonal goals along with strategies for any upcoming competition. In addition, the athlete and coach can plan together the workout for the week and for the 14 day cycle.

As a result of each weekly meeting, specific workouts are written up for a week and posted on the athlete's locker (Fig. 1-6, 1-7).

FIGURE 1-6
SAMPLE
RUNNER'S PROFILE
(14 Day Cycle)

Date **2/3/80**

June Goal Pace **8:52 STEEPLE**

14:10 5000

Date Training Pace **70-71**

Scheduled Meets or Trials 1. **3 MILE ISU MINIDOME**
2. **BIG SKY INDOOR**

Name **DAVE STEFFENS**

Events **STEEPLE - 5000 - 10000**

Cycle Emphasis **POWER**

14 Day Goal Pace **(68-69)**

14:22 3 MILE

Body Weight

Pulse (Resting) **45**

General Evaluation — **lost competition at Logan, Utah ran a 3000 set goal was 8:35 — actual time was 8:31 (6 TH AVERAGE NEW SCHOOL RECORD**

WEIGHTS (2 SETS OF 12)(3 SETS OF 12)(4 SETS, ARMS)(DIPS 20-60)

WEEK # 1

1. **STEADY & FAST 8 MILE**

2. **HILL CIRCUIT FARTLEK**

3. **EASY**

4. **LONG MEDIUM**

5. **PROTEST HILL 3 SETS (DROP DOWN)**

6. **LYDIARD FARTLEK**

7. **LONG EASY**

WEEK # 2

1. **(880 @ 70 DATE PACE × 4) 4 × 330 - DROP DOWN SLIGHT)**

2. **EASY**

3. **STEADY FAST 6 MILE**

4. **HOMER FARTLEK**

5. **EASY**

6. **COMPETE 3 MILES GOAL 14:22**

7. **RECOVERY**

NOTE, DAVE RAN 14:02 AT BIG SKY INDOOR

FIGURE 1-7
SAMPLE
WEEKLY WORKOUT SHEET
For Distance & Middle Distance Runners

NAME: DATE:

Steady warm-up running
a. 2 miles
b. 3 miles
c. 4 miles

2. **Accelerations**
a. (warm-up)
b. drop down—20-70-20

3. **Fartlek**
a. varied (1) 30 min (2)
b. steady (1) 7-10 miles (2)

4. **High knee drills**

5. **Fast sprinter drill**

6. **Stadium stairs**

7. **Intervals**

a. mile	g. 500	m. 150
b. 1320	h. 440	n. 110
c. 100	i. 352	o.
d. 880	j. 330	p.
e. 660	k. 220	q.
f. 550	l. 165	

8. **Ladders**

9. **Hill training**
a. up
b. down
c. up & down
Drills
a. spring-float-spring
b. 30-40-30
c. 35-45-35
d.
e.
f. 70-90-70

11. **Drop downs**
(Distance same letters as #7)

12. **Plyometrics**

13. **Overdistance running**
a.
b. 1.5-2 hours

14. **Weights**

a. general	c. circuit
b. power sets	d. rehabilitation

15. **Trial run**
a. Full effort
b. ¾ effort

16. **Steeple barriers**
a. water jump
b. barriers   Comments:
c. hurdles

17. **Relay exchanges**

18. **Meet with Coach**

19. **Swimming pool**
a. swimming
b. running intervals in shallow water
c. running intervals in deep water

20. **Workout of your choice**

21. **Film study**

M

Tu

W

Th

F

S
Sa

S

Comments:

2

Understanding Strength Training

The athlete must remember that, although extremely important for ultimate performance, weight (strength) training is never the end product. It is only one of the several components necessary for eventual success as a track and field athlete.

There are many ways to lift weights and develop strength and power. Certainly the benefits will differ with the individual programs.

Depending on event and time of the year, each athlete will be placed into one of the following types of programs:

1. Pure Strength and Bulk: heavy loads and limited repetition of 3-5
2. Power Strength (power is the term given to speed, strength and strength endurance): medium repetitions of approximately 5-10 with loading usually not to exceed 75% of maximum
3. Muscle Endurance: light loads of 40-60% of maximum and high repetitions of 12-20

Physiological Considerations Of Strength Training

Hypertrophy (strength gain) occurs with regular overload type activity. Strength gains are demonstrated through four physiological phenomenon:

1. Increasing the amount of protein in the myofibrils. Myofibrils are

the tiny bundles of fibers composed of actin and myosin. Protein synthesis can only occur through bodily need in situations such as growth, injury, and overload training. All of these are dictated by the production of anabolic hormones in the body.

2. Toughening and strengthening of the sarcolemma. The sarcolemma is the connective wall that surrounds the individual protein fibrils. During overload training, these thicken, adding to the tensil strength of each muscle component.

3. Increasing the number of usable capillaries to the muscle. It has been demonstrated in experimental animals that high repetitive activity will stimulate the development of 40% additional blood capillaries. Remember, only high repetition movement causes capillarization. Low reps and heavy weights will not benefit circulatory development.

4. Increasing or re-establishing the elastic strength components of the nervous system. Those activities which elicit the strength reflex will gradually increase not only stretchability, but also contractility (see section on plyometrics).

Training White And Red Muscle Fibers

Recently there has been much talk about the red and white type muscle fibers. The red fibers are considered to determine endurance and white are considered to be the speed-related fibers. It is known that an effective endurance runner must possess nearly 60% red type fibers and a sprinter must have a high percentage of white muscle fiber.

During the early 1970s, Swedish physiologists categorized muscle fibers as being either slow twitch (endurance) or fast twitch (speed). More importantly during these investigations, it was determined that the percentage distribution of the slow twitch and fast twitch varied within one muscle or different muscles of the same individual. In addition, it was found that the oxidative characteristics of individual fibers or muscles could be altered by a type of physical training.

The problem for coaches and athletes is to develop a training routine that causes hypertrophy of special muscle types for special activity, especially those of a speed nature. Evidently, the key is depletion (through fatigue) of available glycogen in a muscle. Both the slow twitch and fast twitch muscles contain quantities of stored glycogen. In general, prolonged exercise depletes the glycogen supply in the slow twitch muscle first. At the point of fatigue of the slow twitch group, the muscle will automatically switch over to the fast twitch characteristics. Only at this stage of activity can we expect hypertrophy of the fast twitch muscle fibers.

Researchers indicate that intensity of exercise is the prime requisite of fast twitch development. Intensity then leads us to believe moderate to heavy weights are the criterion to elicit strength in the fast twitch fiber. From the above information, it is possible to prescribe a definite regimen that will develop the all important fast twitch muscle fiber. First, we wish to deplete glycogen concentration of the slow twitch fiber by beginning an exercise with fairly high repetitions (12-20) and with a light weight (45-55% of max). During successive sets of the exercise, we increase the percentage and still maintain the high repetitions. Midway through the sets, we increase the weight and lift a maximum number of repetitions (lift until you cannot get another repetition). This "burn-out" approach provides the necessary intensity during a time the muscle is fatigued. An example of the concept is:

Exercise	Weight	Set	Repetitions
Bench Press	45% of max	#1	15
	50	#2	12-15
	55%	#3	12
	60%	#4	Maximum number
	65%	#5	Maximum number
	70%	#6	Maximum number

Specifics To Know Concerning Power Training

- **Speed of Repetition:** A fast jerky movement applies force only to a small portion (usually at the start or end of the repetition). In fast movements, the weight is actually lifting the arms. THIS IS BAD!
  A rule of thumb: Take one to two seconds to raise the weight (concentric) and slightly longer to lower the weight (eccentric).
- **Pre-Stretching:** Occurs when a muscle is pulled into a position of increased tension prior to the contraction. This will develop the muscle further as it becomes stronger through the stretch reflex (the principle behind negative resistance and plyometric training).
- **Negative Resistance:** Allows more force and allows for the pre-stretch. This should always be a means of lifting for the hamstrings. Both legs should bring the heavy weight up (concentric) and lower it (eccentric) with only one leg (bring it down slowly).
- **Strength the Criteria:** The amount of work performed in a short period of time (lifting session) is always the best. The nervous threshold is kept high.
- **Central Nervous System Inhibition and Golgi Tendon Apparatus:** This system is set in stages or goals. Opposite muscle groups must

keep a strength gain relationship or ratio with the prime mover. A shot putter must have strong biceps as well as triceps. The hamstrings of a sprinter must keep pace with the quadriceps. To become fast in competition, you must train fast. This allows central nerve impulse adjustment as well as muscle adjustment.

- **Rate of Strength Gain:** Generally, you should expect 5% gain each week - 50% in 7 weeks and 100% in 13 weeks. It will take approximately 6 weeks for a foundation of strength to occur.
- **Maintaining Strength during Competitive Season:** A given level of strength may be maintained at a desired specific level by two maximal contractions per week. IT TAKES NO MORE THAN THIS.
- **Strength Training Is an Energizing Factor:** Decline of the functional state of the central nervous system occurs after exhaustion from any skill training, i.e., high jumping, shot putting, or running. We now know that it takes approximately 24 hours for the nervous system to return to normal. However, through strength training, the athlete is able to recover faster. He will recover even more quickly if it is combined with exercises of low intensity such as running or jogging. Strength exercises as a stimulating factor should be used at all stages of training, including the competitive season.
- **Relate Training with Event - Training for What?:**
  A. Basic Strength
  B. Basic Power
  C. Imitative Power Exercises
  D. Actual Performance

A means to gear program progressions:

Strength	Speed Of Training	Relationship To Actual Event
100%	10%	5%
50%	50%	50%
25%	75%	75%
5%	100%	100%

General Lifting Systems

There have been many successful lifting programs developed and seemingly there is no single program that provides all the benefits necessary in strength development. However, most successful systems fall into one or all of the following lifting systems.

1. **3 X 10** - perform each exercise 10 times, then go through three complete sets. When beginning each new set, add 5 pounds of weight.

2. **Work-up** - Work one muscle group continuously.

    Exp. 10-12 - 200 lbs
          6- 8 - 210 lbs
          4- 6 - 220 lbs
            1 - 240 lbs

This type seems to provide great strength gain without greatly increasing body weight. Therefore it is very good for most track and field events.

3. **Workdown**

    Exp. 10 X 70 lbs
          As many as possible with 60 lbs
          As many as possible with 50 lbs
          As many as possible with 40 lbs

4. **Heavy Light**

    Exp. 4 X Max
          8 X 25 lbs (less than max)

Plyometric Strength Training

Specific participation in the sprints, hurdles, jumps and throws evidently requires more than what is accomplished in the accepted modes of training, i.e., skill technique and general progressive weight training.

Recent studies on the neuro-muscular responses of negative and re-coil stretch training were reported from the USSR. There is evidence that not only were the European jumpers and throwers utilizing plyo-metric exercises, but even the great Russian sprinter, Valery Borzov, underwent extensive plyometric work.

According to the available data, plyometric or depth training prepares the muscles to react under event-like conditions of fast muscular move-ment through eccentric contraction (muscular contraction during the stretch phase). Specifically, plyometrics require the muscle nerve to react and respond to a compressing kinetic action from a position of power and balance while movement is occurring in one direction to an explosive opposite movement. This action of stretch to movement is directed by the very complex golgi tendon apparatus in the muscle.

In practice, plyometric conditioning occurs in two ways; first, when an athlete overcomes kinetic energy of his falling body (such as jumping down from a high box and recoiling upward); second when a body seg-ment is loaded, stretched eccentrically and immediately impelled to a change direction (such as a baseball player swinging his bat back-wards prior to the forward swing, effecting a braking action and an eccentric stretch). "The capability of producing a stronger following (subsequent) concentric muscular contraction by utilizing a previous eccentric contraction of that muscle is known as the stretch or myotic reflex."[1]

It should be noted when developing training schedules and programs that speed-strength increases show best results when they occur **without** loading the body or body segments. Loading will increase maximum strength, but will slow down the nerve muscle response.

How The Plyometric Principle Works

Plyometric training, or in-depth training, is basically the stopping or braking of one motion followed by a forceful movement in the opposite direction. This action serves as an immediate stretch reflex which produces extra muscular contraction. Take, for example, an elastic band. Stretch it slightly and it will recoil slightly, stretch it nearly to the breaking point and it will recoil with much additional force.

Generally the typical athlete who trains in a typical program is trained for strength in the following manner: bulk, which simply increases the cross sectional size of the muscle mass; general strength, the development of static and dynamic muscular involvement; power, the development of explosive strength and strength movement; and, finally, muscular endurance, the ability to sustain rapid muscular action over long periods of time.

As we analyze the foregoing and the completed product (the competitive athlete), we find that many athletes have tremendous strength yet cannot convert this strength into movement. As Fred Wilt states, athletes "fail to bridge the gap between sheer strength and power." Depth jumping or plyometric exercises seem to be the available bridge for this gap.

Physiologists now realize that a loaded muscle going through concentric contraction is *much* more powerful following an eccentric prestretch phase. In our basic training routines, we invariably overlook not only the eccentric contractions but even more of the pre-stretch. The faster a muscle is forced to lengthen, the greater the tension exerted. It is necessary to remember here that rate (speed or time) is indeed more important than magnitude (length of stretch).

You will note that the successful flop high jumper needs to shorten his step prior to take-off. During this shorter phase, great tension is created over a *shorter* period of time which as a result provides impulse upward. Force plates have been used to compare the straddle jumper

---

[1]Wilt, Fred. "Plyometrics, What It Is and How It Works", **Athletic Journal**, Vol. 55, May 1975.

and the flopper during the impulse of take-off. The flopper has a distinct advantage here over our time-honored "power x time long last step" of the straddle jumper.

Fred Wilt provides the following guidelines for plyometric training when developing programs for the athlete:

- Maximum tension develops when the active muscle is stretched quickly.
- The faster a muscle is forced to lengthen, the greater the tension it exerts.
- The rate of stretch is more important than the magnitude of stretch.
- Utilize the overload principle, which specifies that increased strength of a muscle results only from work at an intensity greater than that to which it is accustomed.

Plyometric training differs from the normal program in weight training with regard to recovery rates. Generally, for the prepared or previously trained athlete, duration and frequency of in-depth work can exceed the amount of performance of the novice. For the beginner, one session per week is sufficient, and for the advanced, a maximum of two sessions per week would be sufficient.

Interestingly, the best recovery device is a general weight training session with moderate loading immediately following a plyometric session. It is best to train through plyometrics by supplementing speed and strength sessions together and not strength alone.

If there is to be important skill training for an event, plyometric training should preceed it by three days and even four days may be necessary for complete recovery. After a heavy depth jumping session, it may be necessary to give the athlete 8-10 days before going into an important competition. This type of training tends to slow the nerve muscle response temporarily. Follow a day of heavy plyometrics with general endurance or easy tempo running.

A sprinter's program would include the use of very fast hopping on one leg, then both legs, for distances of 30-60 yards for the development of explosive starting potential. Slower bounding and hopping for the same distances will build speed endurance potential.

For best results, the sprinters should use the shorter and more intensive hopping before actual sprint training and use the longer hopping drills after sprint training the following day.

Type Of Exercises Used To Stimulate The Stretch Response Principle And Eccentric Muscular Contraction

BOXES - 40", 30", 18", 12", 6", 3", 2"

   A - Single and Double Leg Hopping - box to ground to box

   B - Step off box; jump as high as possible

   C - Off box to ground to long jump, triple jump or high jump, or off box to shot throwing position

   D - Off ground to box to long jump, triple jump or high jump

   E - Lateral bench hopping; for thirty seconds hop with both feet as many repetitions as possible from one side to the other side of the bench or box; stress quick impulse actions of the arms driving no higher than the chin.

HURDLES

   A - Double leg hopping over varied heights of hurdles set approximately 3-4 yards apart.

   B - Jump turn over hurdle, making 180° turn and repeat

   C - Single leg hopping over varied heights of hurdles

STADIUM STAIRS

   A - Double or single leg hopping up stairs (usually skip a step or go seat to seat)

   B - Double or single leg hopping down

FLAT DRILLS

   A - Progressive squat jumps

   B - Hopping backwards on power leg

   C - Standing long and triple jump

   D - Backward standing long jump

   E - One legged squat jumps

   F - Bounding vertically on spot for 30-60 seconds

   G - Bounding or hopping over short distances

   H - Box to low **slow** squat to another box

Selected Strength Training Programs

The descriptive strength training program that follows is aimed at total physiological development over a ten month period. Not only should the reader consider these formal weight training activities, but s/he should also remember that many other supplemental activities must support and assist in an athlete's overall strength development. Supplemental activities should include: power strength techniques, such as up hill and stair sprinting; elastic speed and strength, developed by bounding, hopping, and depth jumping; nerve-speed techniques, which are developed by assisted running and down hill training. In the development of any specific strength programs, one should consider the length of the competitive season, the number of competitions per month, the need for peaking, and the time and facilities available for training.

The following strength training programs have evolved from Bulgaria and other Eastern European countries whose national and international weight lifting teams have experienced unusual success with their strength training methods.

Sprinters And Hurdlers
Weight Training Sequence

I. Initial Prep & Testing Cycle (Sept. 4 - Oct. 9) (3 units/week)
MON-WED-FRI

	Exercises	System
Week 1-3	Warm-up & Skill Activities	
	1. Lateral Bench Hops x 3	3 x 20
	2. Alternate Dumbbell Curls	3 x 20
	3. Good Morning	1 x 30
	4. Extension Sit-ups or Hanging Leg Lifts	
	5. Back Arches	1 x -
	Strength & Skill Lifts	
	1. Double Squats (1 Day/Week Inverted Leg Press)	3 x 15
	2. Clean & Jerk	3 x 15
	3. Step-ups	3 x 15 each leg
	4. Hamstrings (Mon-Fri Reg. - Wed Negative)	
	5. Bench or Incline Press	3 x 15
	6. Quadriceps (only if muscle imbalance exists)	3 x 15 weak leg

Friday, Week 3 - Test for Max

	Mon	**Wed**	**Fri**
Week 4	40-45-55-60%	45-50-55-60-65%	50-55-60-65-70%
Week 5	55-60-65-70-75%	60-65-70-75-80%	55-60-65-70-75%
Week 6	60-65-70-75-80%	65-70-75-80-85%	Test Max on Squats, Clean & Jerk, Hamstrings, Bench or Incline, Bench Hop

First two sets 10-15 reps, remaining sets as many reps as possible

II. **Specific Prep Cycle** (Oct. 12 - Nov. 13) (3 Units/Week)
Goal: Endurance Strength Capillarization

	Mon	Wed	Fri
Week 1	55-60-65-70-75%	60-65-70-75-80%	55-60-65-70-75%
Week 2	60-65-70-75-80%	65-70-75-80-85%	60-65-70-75-80%
Week 3	65-70-75-80-85%	70-75-80-85-90%	65-70-75-80-85%
Week 4	70-75-80-85-90%	75-80-85-90-95%	70-75-80-85-90%
Week 5	75-80-85-90-95%	80-85-90-95-100%	Test for Max

First two sets 10-15 reps, remaining sets as many as possible

III. **Transfer Cycle** (Nov. 16 - Dec. 18)
GOALS: Transfer Power to Impulse
All Lifts As Fast & Powerful As Possible

Exercises

Squats
Clean & Jerk
Step-ups
Bench or Incline Press
Low Split Cleans (Both Leg Lead)
Dead Lifts (Start Light Increase Load)

Hamstrings; Negative Only
NOT FAST!; But Heavy

	Tues	Thurs
Week 1	3-5 @ 80% x 3-5	3-5 @ 70% x 3-5
Week 2	3-5 @ 75% x 3-5	3-5 @ 50% x 3-5
Week 3	3-5 @ 75% x 3-5	3-5 @ 70% x 3-5
Week 4	6 @ 80% x 6	Test for Max

IV. **Cluster Cycle** (Jan. 4 - Feb. 12)
GOALS: Facilitation & Energy Reserve (All Lifts Done at 90% or Above)

Mon-Wed-Fri (When Not Traveling)

Week 1-6		
1/2 Squat	3 reps x 3 sets x 3 bunches	30-45 secs between
Power Clean	1 rep x 5 sets x 2 bunches	sets and 1½ minutes
Low Split Clean	1 rep x 5 sets x 2 bunches	between bunches.
Step-ups	5 reps x 3 sets x 3 bunches	
Bench Press	3 reps x 3 sets x 3 bunches	
Hanging Leg-ups	5 reps x 5 sets x 5 bunches	
Hamstrings	5 reps x 5 sets x 5 bunches	

V. **Competitive cycle I** (Feb. 15 - Mar. 26)

	Mon	Wed
Week 1	5 x 5 @ 60%	5 x 5 @ 60%
Week 2	5 x 5 @ 70%	5 x 5 @ 75%
Week 3	5 x 5 @ 75%	5 x 5 @ 80%
Week 4	70-75-80-85%	85-90-95%
Week 5	5 x 5 @ 70%	5 x 4 @ 80%
Week 6	5 x 6 @ 60%	5 x 4 @ 70%

VI. **Competitive Cycle II** (Mar. 28 - Apr. 30)

	Mon	Wed
Week 1	4 x 3 @ 75%	5 x 3 @ 85%
Week 2	70-75-80-85%	75-80-85-90-95%
Week 3	4 x 3 @ 75%	3 x 3 @ 85%
Week 4	4 x 3 @ 75%	2 x 3 @ 90%

VII. **Maintenance & Peak Cycle** (May 3 - June ?)

Mon	Wed
4 of 5 @ 90%	4 of 5 @ 60%
4 of 5 @ 95%	4 of 5 @ 70%
3 of 5 @ 90%	3 of 5 @ 75%

Jumpers Weight Training Sequence

I. Initial Prep & Testing Cycle (Sept. 4 - Oct. 9) (3 Units/Week)
GOALS: A. Muscle Balance
B. Hypertrophy - Tendon Development

MON-WED-FRI

	Exercises	System
Week 1-3	Clean & Jerk	3 x 15
	Double Squats	3 x 15
	Step-Ups	3 x 15
	Quads	3 x 15
	Hamstrings	3 x 15 (1 day/wk neg. res.)
	Lateral Bench	3 to 20 secs.
	Incline Bench	3 x 15
	Incline Sit-Up	3 x 20
	Heel Raisers	3 x 60
	Toe Raisers with Tube	3 x 60

Friday, Week 3 - Test for Max - 3 rep

	Mon	Wed	Fri
Week 4	40-45-55-60%	45-50-55-60-65%	50-55-60-65-70%
Week 5	55-60-65-70-75%	60-65-70-75-80%	55-60-65-70-75%
Week 6	60-65-70-75-80%	65-70-75-8-85%	Test for Max 1 Rep &
	First two sets 10-15 reps	Power Clean Only	
	Remaining sets as many		
	as possible		

II. Specific Prep Cycle (Oct. 12 - Nov. 13) (4 sets - 5-6 reps)
GOAL: Max Strength

	Mon	Tues	Wed
Week 1-5	½ Squat	3 hurdle bounding	Sitting Leg Press
	Inverted Leg Press	10 rep, increase	High Step Ups
	Power Clean	to 5 x 12	Shoulder Curls
	Snatch	Butt Kickers	Skipping
	Dumbbell Curls		Hyperextension Sit-up
	High Step-ups		Hamstrings
	Hamstrings		

Thurs		Fri
Depth Jumping		¼ Squat
2 sets/12 reps L.H.		Inverted Leg Press
1 set/10 reps Stop		Snatch
1 set/15 reps H.H.		Knee-up
		½ Squats
		L-ups from bar
		Hamstrings
		High Step-ups

Last day of 5th week - test
for max.

III. Transfer Cycle (Nov. 16 - Dec. 18)
GOALS:Transfer Power to Impulse
All lifts as fast and explosive as possible

Exercises

Squats
Inverted Leg Press
Split Squats
Jump Squats
Hyperextension Sit-ups
Clean & Jerk

	Mon	**Wed**	**Fri**
Week 1	3-5 @ 80% x 3-5	3-5 @ 70% x 3-5	3-5 @ 50% x 3-5
Week 2	3-5 @ 75% x 3-5	3-5 @ 50% x 3-5	3-5 @ 60% x 3-5
Week 3	3-5 @ 75% x 3-5	3-5 @ 70% x 3-5	3-5 @ 60% x 3-5
Week 4	6 @ 80% x 6	6 @ 70% x 6	Test for Max

IV. Cluster Cycle (Jan. 4 - Feb. 12) Christmas Vacation 2 week break
GOALS: Facilitation and Energy Reserve
Do all lifting in short powerful burst - Yet allow complete recovery between sets. All lifts are done at 90% or above.

MON-WED-FRI

Week 1-6	½ Squat	3 reps x 3 sets x 3 bunches	30-45 secs between
	Inverted Leg Press	2 reps x 3 sets x 3 bunches	sets and 1½ min.
	¼ Squat	2 reps x 3 sets x 3 bunches	between bunches.
	Power Clean	1 rep x 5 sets x 2 bunches	
	Alternate Jump Squats	5 reps x 3 sets x 3 bunches	
	Snatch	1 rep x 5 sets x 2 bunches	
	Sitting Leg Press	2 reps x 5 sets x 3 bunches	
	Leg-ups	5 reps x 5 sets x 5 bunches	
	Low Step-up	2 reps x 3 sets x 3 bunches	

V. Competitive Cycle I Max Strength (Feb. 15 - Mar. 26)

Mon	**Tues**	**Wed**
½ Squats	Hamstrings 3 x 15	¾ Squats
Lateral Bench w/vest	High Step-ups 4 x 20	½ Squat
Inverse Leg Press	Drills	Lateral Bench no vest
Bounding 4 of 5		Bounding 4 of 5
Power Clean		Inverted Leg Press
Hyperex Sit-ups		Snatch
2 x 50		Split Squat Jump
Split Squats 5 x 8		Inclined Bench Press
Dumbbell Curl 3 x 20		

Thurs	**Fri**	**(Fri con't)**
Drills	½ Squat	Hyperextension Sit-ups
Hamstrings (negative)	Lateral Bench Vest	2 x 30
3 x 15	Inverted Leg Press	Split Squat
High Step-ups 3 x 20	Bounding 4-5	Dumbbell Curl or Fly
	Power Clean	Jump
		Low Step-ups

Week 1	5 x 5 x 60%	5 x 5 x 60%	5 x 5 x 70%
Week 2	5 x 5 x 70%	5 x 5 x 75%	5 x 5 x 80%
Week 3	5 x 5 x 75%	5 x 5 x 80%	5 x 5 x 85%
Week 4	70-75-80-85%	85-90-95%	90-95-100%
Week 5	5 x 5 x 70%	5 x 4 x 80%	5 x 6 x 100%
Week 6	5 x 6 x 60%	5 x 4 x 70%	Test for Max

VI. **Competitive Cycle II** (Mar. 28 - Apr. 30)

	Mon	Wed	
Week 1	4 x 3 x 75%	5 x 3 x 85%	Same lifts as Wed.
Week 2	70-75-80-85%	75-80-85-90-95%	and Fri. of competitive
Week 3	4 x 3 x 75%	3 x 3 x 85%	cycle
Week 4	4 x 3 x 75%	75-80-85-90-95%	

V. **Maintenance & Peak Cycle** (May 3 - June ?)
GOAL: To Maintain Strength and Power To The End of Season
Lifting Days Monday and Wednesday Only

Exercises		Sequence	
		Mon.	Wed.
¼ Squats	4 sets of 5	@ 90%	60%
Inverted Leg Press	4 sets of 5	@ 95%	70%
Sitting Leg Press	4 sets of 5	@ 60%	80%
Low Step-up	4 sets of 5	@ 80%	90%

Throwers Selected Exercises

3-4 unit lifting exercises
Basic Strength Program
1. Incline press or bench press
2. ¾ squats
3. Dead lift (1 day per week)
4. Incline flys (lateral arm raise)
Power cleans
Additional 2-Unit Lifting Exercises to be used during a 4 or 5 unit week:
Skill Strength Program
1. Hang snatch
2. Step-ups
3. Press behind neck
4. Bicep curls
5. Single leg supine press
6. Clean and jerk
Warm-up Exercises
1. Jogging-½ to ¾ mile - Lateral bench hops 2 x 20 seconds
2. Hamstring stretch
3. Quadricep stretch
4. Groin stretch
5. Low back stretch
6. Upper back and shoulder stretch (with stick)

General Weight Training Schedule

Weight Events

I. Initial Prep & Testing Cycle (Sept. 10 - Sept. 28) (3 Units/Week)

	Mon	Wed	Fri
Week 1	3 x 15	3 x 15	3 x 15
Week 2	3 x 15	3 x 15	3 x 15
Week 3	3 x 15	3 x 15	Test for Max

II. Specific Prep Cycle (Oct. 1 - Nov. 9) (3 Units/Week)

	Mon	Wed	Fri
Week 1	40-45-50-55%	45-50-55-60%	50-55-60-65-70%
Week 2	55-60-65-70-75%	60-65-70-75-80%	55-60-65-70-75%
Week 3	60-65-70-75-80%	65-70-75-80-85%	60-65-70-75-80%
Week 4	65-70-75-80-85%	70-75-80-85-90%	65-70-75-80-85%
Week 5	70-75-80-85-90%	75-80-85-90-95%	70-75-80-85-90%
Week 6	75-80-85-90-95%	80-85-90-95-100%	Test for Max

III. Transition Cycle (Nov. 12 - Dec. 21) (3 Units/Week)

	Mon	Wed	Fri
Week 1	5 x 5 x 60%	5 x 5 x 40%	5 x 5 x 60%
Week 2	5 x 5 x 65%	5 x 5 x 45%	5 x 5 x 65%
Week 3	5 x 5 x 70%	5 x 5 x 50%	5 x 5 x 70%
Week 4	5 x 5 x 75%	5 x 5 x 60%	5 x 5 x 75%
Week 5	5 x 5 x 80%	5 x 5 x 65%	5 x 5 x 80%
Week 6	5 x 5 x 85%	5 x 5 x 70%	Test for Max

IV. Competitive Phase I (Jan. 7 - Feb. 29) (3 Units/Week)

	Tues	Thurs	Sat or Sun
Week 1	4 x 5 x 75%	6 x 5 x 85%	4 x 3 x 60%
Week 2	3 x 5 x 80%	6 x 5 x 85%	4 x 3 x 60%
Week 3	4 x 70-75-80%	3 x 80-85-90%	Test for Max
Week 4	3 x 70-75-80%	5 x 80-90-95%	4 x 55-60-65%
Week 5	4 x 75-80-85%	3 x 85-90-95%	6 x 60-65-70-75%
Week 6	4 x 70-75-80%	3 x 75-80-85-90-95%	4 x 55-60-65%
Week 7	5 x 5 x 75%	5 x 5 x 60%	5 x 5 x 75%
Week 8	5 x 5 x 80%	5 x 5 x 70%	Test for Max

Strength Training

Proceeding Competition

V. Competitive Phase II (Mar. 3 - April 11) (3 Units/Week)

	Tues	Thurs	Sat or Sun
Week 1	4 x 3 x 75%	5 x 3 x 85%	4 x 3 x 60%
Week 2	4 x 3 x 80%	6 x 3 x 85%	4 x 3 x 60%
Week 3	4 x 3 x 75%	3 x 3 x 85%	4 x 3 x 60%
Week 4	4 x 3 x 80%	1 x 3 x 90%	4 x 3 x 60%
Week 5	4 x 3 x 75%	2 x 3 x 90%	4 x 3 x 60%
Week 6	4 x 3 x 75%	3 x 3 x 90%	Test for Max

VI. Peak Phase (April 14 - May 16) (2 Units/Week)

Week 1	90% Sunday	60% Tuesday
Week 2	Max Effort Sunday	60% Tuesday
Week 3	90% Sunday	60% Tuesday
Week 4	60% Sunday	Rest
Week 5	Prepare for conference	
Week 6		

Distance And Middle Distance Runners Weight And Strength Training Program

More and more we hear of successful coaches putting their runners through some type of vigorous weight training program. We are finding that these athletes not only compete much better, but also are less susceptible to injuries.

As a point of interest, however, many programs incorporate lifting characterized by high reps and low weights. In reviewing, we find that scheme of lifting conducive to red muscle fiber development. Most distance and middle distance runners, through their normal running sessions, have more than enough light load repetitive movements.

White muscle fiber development is really what the distance and middle distance runners lack. The white fibers provide strength, power and speed components, thus providing development to those physiological areas not usually trained.

With this in mind, a functional program will consist of sets of 5-6 with the repetition being between 6-8. The amount of weight is set by a maximum lift test through a variety of lifting exercises. The lifting weight would begin in the area of 45% and go to around 70% for the final set. Approximately every 5 weeks, a new maximum should be established.

Selected Lifts
1. Military press (either seated or standing)
2. Bent over rowing
3. Bicep curl or dumbbell curls
4. Hanging clean and jerk
5. Upright rowing

The lifting days will vary as the athlete goes through his or her hard and easy day running program. Lifting days should be on the easy running day. During the lifting session, the athlete should strive for a "quick" weight training session lasting for a maximum of 30 minutes. The runner should also attempt to finish this lifting session with stretching and light running.

Weight Training Record

NAME _____ **DATE**

EVENT _____

Selected Exercise	One Rep. Maximum	(Date)	(Date)	(Date)	(Date)
1.	_____	_____	_____	_____	_____
2.	_____	_____	_____	_____	_____
3.	_____	_____	_____	_____	_____
4.	_____	_____	_____	_____	_____
5.	_____	_____	_____	_____	_____
6.	_____	_____	_____	_____	_____
7.	_____	_____	_____	_____	_____
8.	_____	_____	_____	_____	_____
9.	_____	_____	_____	_____	_____
Body Wt._____ Tot. Lb.	_____	_____	_____	_____	_____

Height_____

	Date	Date
Bicep	_____	_____
Thigh	_____	_____
Waist	_____	_____
Buttocks	_____	_____
Calf	_____	_____

Hamstring Quad Strength

	H	(L)	(R)	Q	(L)	(R)
Date		_____	_____		_____	_____
Date		_____	_____		_____	_____
Date		_____	_____		_____	_____
Date		_____	_____		_____	_____

Weight Training Percentage Table

Rounded To 5 Pounds

Wt.	40%	45%	50%	55%	60%	65%	70%	75%	80%	85%	90%	95%
50	20	25	25	30	30	35	35	40	40	45	45	45
60	25	30	30	35	35	40	40	45	50	55	55	55
70	30	35	35	40	40	50	50	55	55	60	60	65
80	30	40	45	50	50	55	60	65	70	70	75	
90	35	40	45	50	55	60	65	65	75	80	80	85
100	40	45	50	55	60	65	70	75	80	85	90	95
110	45	50	55	60	65	70	75	85	90	95	100	105
120	50	55	60	65	70	80	85	90	95	100	110	115
130	55	60	65	70	80	85	90	100	105	110	115	125
140	55	65	70	75	85	90	100	105	110	120	125	135
150	60	70	75	85	90	100	105	115	120	130	135	145
160	65	75	80	90	95	105	110	120	130	135	145	150
170	70	80	85	95	100	1101	120	125	135	145	155	160
180	70	80	90	100	110	115	125	135	145	155	160	170
190	75	85	90	105	115	125	135	145	150	160	170	180
200	80	90	100	1101	120	130	140	150	160	1701	180	190
210	85	100	105	115	125	135	145	155	170	180	190	190
220	90	100	110	120	130	145	155	165	175	185	200	210
230	95	105	115	125	140	150	160	175	185	195	205	220
240	95	110	120	130	145	155	170	180	190	205	215	230
250	100	115	125	140	150	165	175	190	200	215	225	240
260	105	120	130	145	155	170	180	195	210	220	235	245
270	110	125	135	150	160	175	190	200	215	230	245	255
280	110	125	140	155	170	180	195	210	225	240	250	265
290	115	130	145	160	175	190	205	220	230	245	260	270
300	120	135	150	165	180	195	210	225	240	255	270	285
310	125	140	155	1701	185	200	215	230	250	265	280	295
320	130	145	160	175	190	210	225	240	255	270	290	305
330	135	150	165	180	200	215	230	250	265	2801	300	315
350	145	160	175	195	210	230	245	265	280	300	315	335
360	140	160	190	200	220	230	250	270	290	310	320	340
390	160	180	200	210	230	250	270	290	310	330	350	370
420	170	190	210	230	250	270	290	320	340	360	380	400
450	180	200	230	250	270	290	320	340	360	380	410	430
480	190	220	240	260	290	310	340	360	380	410	430	460
510	200	230	260	280	310	330	360	380	410	430	460	490
540	220	240	270	300	320	350	380	410	430	460	490	510
570	230	260	290	310	340	370	400	430	460	480	510	540
600	240	270	300	330	360	390	420	450	480	510	540	570

Weight Training For The Decathlon

By Bill Bakley

With so many events in which to participate, the decathlete has to be strong throughout his entire body. One part cannot be overlooked. A decathlete cannot lift like a single event performer, he must lift for all the events, which can create a problem. A four-phase program that works all the necessary muscle groups must be developed.

The Decathlete should be strong throughout his entire body.

The first phase builds endurance and strength. This phase lasts 12 weeks with four workouts per week. The major emphasis is on creating endurance in the muscle groups. As the decathlete begins this program, a light weight should be chosen to perform the entire workout. The muscle groups will increase in strength and size, even with the use of light to moderate weights. As strength and endurance increase, small weight increases can take place, but no more than 10 pounds per week.

Phase One (Endurance/Strength)
Day 1 & 4

	(sets/reps)	(wts)
1. Upright Rowing	6x6	( )
2. Lat Pulldowns	6x6	( )
3. Bent-over Rowing	6x6	( )
4. Deadlift	4x6	( )
5. Press	6x6	( )
6. Behind Neck Press	6x6	( )
7. Front Raises (db)	4x12	( )
8. Side Raises (db)	4x12	( )
9. Bent-over Raises (db)	4x12	( )
10. Triceps	6x6	( )
11. Biceps	6x6	( )
12. Incline Situps		( )

Day 2 & 5

		(wts)
1. Squats	15	( )
	6x6	( )
2. Lunges	4x8	( )
3. Quads	6x6	( )
4. Hamstrings	6x6	( )
5. Hip Flexors	6x12	( )
6. Flies (db)	6x6	( )
7. Bench Press	15	( )
	6x6	( )
8. Incline Bench	6x4	( )
Pullovers	6x6	( )
10. Incline Situps		( )
11. Toe Raises	5x12	( )

The second phase starts the transition into the power phase. While there is no power lifting, weights are increased and the number of sets and repetitions performed for any given exercise are decreased. This second phase lasts 12 weeks. The major emphasis is on developing strength for power lifting. As strength increases, the weight being lifted will increase. A five pound increase every two weeks is standard for most lifts involving the upper body. With the lower body lifts, a 10-15 pound increase every two weeks is common. During this phase, a plateau may be reached. To get past this "stalling point," drop the weight down and increase one to two sets to develop more endurance. After a week of performing at this lower weight, increase the weight and return to the number of sets being performed at the time the plateau was reached.

Twelve weeks after starting this phase increased muscle size and strength will be noticed. Keep in mind that stress placed upon the muscle groups must increase continuously to create strength and size gains.

Phase Two (Strength)
Day 1 & 4

	(sets/reps)	(wts)
1. Upright Rowing	4x6	( )
2. Lat Pulldowns	4x6	( )
3. Bent-over Rowing	4x6	( )
4. Deadlift	3x6	( )
5. Press	4x6	( )
6. Behind Neck Press	4x6	( )
7. Front Raises (db)	3x12	( )
8. Side Raises (db)	3x12	( )
9. Bent-over Raises (db)	3x12	( )
10. Triceps	5x6	( )
11. Biceps	5x6	( )
12. Incline Situps		( )

Day 2 & 5

1. Squats	15	( )
	4x6	( )
2. Lunges	4x8	( )
3. Quads	4x6	( )
4. Hamstrings	4x6	( )
5. Hip Flexors	4x12	( )
6. Flies (db)	4x6	( )
7. Bench Press	15	( )
	4x6	( )
8. Incline Bench	4x4	( )
9. Pullovers	4x6	( )
10. Incline Situps		( )
11. Toe Raises	4x12	( )

The third phase of the weight training program completes the transition to power lifting. During this phase exercises are performed three days per week, one day of power and two days of building. The workouts on the building days are done with moderately heavy weights. These weights increase from phase two, but at a slower rate. Power lifting is performed with heavy weight, up to 95% of maximum, on the upper body area. The lower body power lifting takes place in the fourth phase. The reasoning behind this is that more time is needed for upper body development than for the lower body. The lower body usually responds quickly to heavy weights and will have plenty of time to develop in the fourth phase of lifting. In addition, much of the lower body development takes place through running, hills and jump drills.

Phase Three (Strength/Power)
Day 1

	(sets/reps)	(wts)
1. Upright Rowing	3x6	( )
2. Lat Pulldowns	3x6	( )
3. Bent-over Rowing	3x6	( )
4. Deadlift	3x3	( )
5. Press	3x6	( )
6. Behind Neck Press	3x6	( )
7. Front Raises (db)	3x8	( )
8. Side Raises (db)	3x8	( )
9. Bent-over Raises (db)	3x8	( )
10. Triceps	3x6	( )
11. Biceps	3x6	( )
12. Incline Situps		( )

Day 2 & 5

1. Squats	15	( )
	8	( )
	4x4	( )
2. Lunges	4x8	( )
3. Quads	4x8	( )
4. Hamstrings	3x6	( )
5. Hip Flexors	3x12	( )
6. Flies (db)	3x6	( )
7. Bench Press	15	( )
	4x6	( )
8. Incline Bench	4x3	( )
9. Pullovers	4x6	( )
10. Incline Situps		( )
11. Toe Raises	3x12	( )

Day 4

1. Bench	10	(	)
	5x2	(	)
2. Incline Bench	6	(	)
	4x3	(	)
3. Clean & Jerk	4	(	)
	4x2	(	)
4. Triceps	2x6	(	)
5. Biceps	2x6	(	)
6. Situps		(	)

The fourth phase of lifting is the all-power stage that includes one day of power for the upper body, one day of power for the lower body and one day of maintenance for the smaller muscle groups. This final phase lasts for the balance of the season. The maintenance day may be used as a pre-meet warm up (2 days before) if the power lifting conflicts with a meet. On the power days, the lifts should be done at 95% to 100% of maximum. Every week there should be a weight increase, at least 5 pounds on most exercises. While exercising triceps, biceps, quads and hamstrings, one should be careful not to exceed a point where tearing or joint soreness occurs. These exercises may not show an increase in weight at a certain point.

Phase Four (Power)
Day 1

	(sets/reps)	(wts)	
1. Bench	10	(	)
	5x2	(	)
2. Incline Bench	6	(	)
	4x3	(	)
3. Clean & Jerk	4	(	)
	5x2	(	)
4. Triceps	3x6	(	)
5. Biceps	3x6	(	)
6. Situps		(	)

Day 3

1. Squats	15	(	)
	8	(	)
	7x2	(	)
2. Lunges	4x8	(	)
3. Quads	3x6	(	)
4. Hamstrings	3x6	(	)

5. Hip Flexors	3x12	(	)
6. Incline Situps		(	)
7. Toe Raises	3x12	(	)

Day 5

1. Upright Rowing	2x6	(	)
2. Lat Pulldowns	2x6	(	)
3. Bent-over Rowing	2x6	(	)
4. Deadlift	2x3	(	)
5. Press	2x6	(	)
6. Behind Neck Press	2x6	(	)
7. Front Raises (db)	1x8	(	)
8. Side Raises (db)	1x8	(	)
9. Bent-over Raises (db)	1x8	(	)
10. Flies (db)	2x6	(	)
11. Triceps	3x6	(	)
12. Biceps	3x6	(	)
13. Incline Situps		(	)

This four-phase lifting program provides a well developed plan for each muscle group and stage needed throughout the year. By using this program for one year, large strength and power increases should be noticed.

3

Posture and Mechanics for Efficient Running

Posture and Mechanics for Efficient Running

Before I delve too far into some of the technicalities of posture and body carriage in running, I feel compelled to advise the student of unacceptable attitudes in running form. It is impossible and completely inadvisable for athletes to fit themselves into a mold of so-called "proper form." Each person has a unique skeletal and muscular system. Therefore, each must seek their own correct style, efficiency and comfort.

Balance Problems

Body problems in running are actually created by motion itself. As a rule, while simply standing an individual has little or no postural problems; improper body posture causes fatigue, tension and eventual discomfort, forcing a change to a more comfortable position.

Motion, on the other hand, upsets the tension-relief cycle. To best portray the problem, think of a pop-bottle sitting upright on a skate board. If you initiate a quick pull (acceleration) upon the skate board, the bottom portion of the bottle begins movement before the top half. Therefore, as more acceleration is applied to the skate board, the bottle falls over in a direction opposite to the moving board. On the other hand, if we place a wedge under the bottle on the back side so that it has a pronounced forward lean (in the direction of the moving skate board), then acceleration must be greater to make the bottle fall backwards. By studying the bottle stability, we learn that the faster the acceleration upon the board, the more pronounced the lean should be upon the bottle to prevent it from tipping. Further complications are added by the height of the bottle. The taller the bottle, the less stable, and the shorter the bottle, the more stable. These items both relate to the amount of forward lean in insuring stability.

Running upsets stability, but on the other hand forward lean restores it. When a runner accelerates, that forward lean needs to be more pronounced. As the speed becomes constant, the body assumes a more upright position. In other words, the runner must adjust to acceleration continually by noticeable body displacement. The important thing to remember is body lean changes under periods of acceleration or deacceleration, i.e. at the start, middle, and finish of the race.

However, pickup acceleration during the middle of a race need not be noticeable by the so-called upper body lean. This can be correctly and naturally absorbed by the simple adjustment of center of gravity in the area of the pelvis (hips). This allows the runner to adapt without any change in body lean.

The Importance of the Arms in Running

There seems to be an issue between coaches as to the effectiviness of runners deliberately using the arms to change posture and running style. Many agree that the arms are the determining factor to maintain a speed ratio. On the other hand, the legs are simply the resultant factors which are dependent upon the speed ratio of the arms. Others say if a runner is obsessed with arms action, he should try running on his hands.

Regardless of the stand taken, we have some interesting ideas about arm carriage and action relationship to running styles. The student of running must never loose sight of the fact that running is a total body effort.

Arm adjustment influences a runner's body lean, stride length, and, more important, his ability to perform well.

Generally speaking, the rate of arm speed will be consistent with the rate of leg speed. Running, as well as walking, is a coordinated effort of both the legs and the arms. This action and counteraction serve to compliment one another. The actual function of the coordinating arm swing is not only to develop a source of power of force but is a means of absorbing the unwanted rotation produced by locomotion. Therefore,

FIGURE 3-1

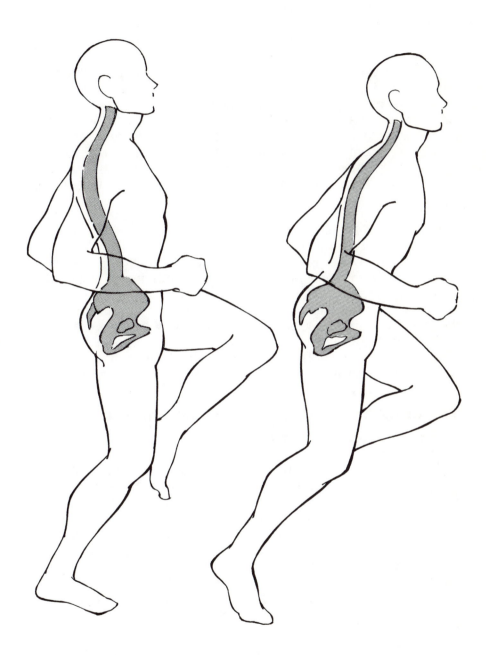

1A   1B

each movement of the leg, whether characterized by the long, powerful stride of a sprinter or the somewhat shortened, smooth stride of a distance runner, must be initated by the arms, or undue body contortions will be evident.

In contrast to leg action, similar changes in arm activity change leg movement and overall body posture as well. For example, a distance runner usually wishes to carry the arms high and in close to the chest and body for three reasons: (1) it allows less weight to be carried by the upper body due to leverages; (2) it places less strain upon the circulatory system as the blood flow through the arms returns to the heart by gravity rather than a complete dependence upon the heart; and (3) it allows the efficient upright posture important in all types of running. The sprinter, on the other hand, reaches out during running, thus giving a longer power phase and float phase characteristic of the fast moving runner.

An interesting question is: how much across-the-body action of the arms is necessary for an efficient runner? Naturally, we know that a distance runner's arms will have more crosswise action due to his holding them in near the body with the elbows out, whereas, there seems to be a misconception that he only allows the arms to swing forward and backward. Common instructions indicate that there should be no across-the-chest motions. To test the validity of this statement, flex the arms at the elbow to 90 degrees, relax and allow the arms to swing to the front and to the rear. Where do they naturally go? Across the chest to the mid line or sternum. This too, is the case in distance running as well as sprinting. It is never good to allow the arms to move across the midline of the body in any kind of running.

The Arms as a Means of Providing Impulse

In addition to coordinating movement with the legs, the arms used in proper fashion can provide a great deal of impulse (transferrence of force) into and away from the ground. Newton's Third Law states "for every action there is an opposite and equal reaction." The forward and backward motion of the arms during a running stride is no exception to that law. This reaction can be maximized by instructing the sprinter to block (stop) very quickly both the to and fro arm action. The forward arm block directs impulse into the ground, and the backward block directs impulse from the ground into the runner. Examples of this arm action can be seen in photo sequence of John Carlos #3-7, 3-8, 3-9 (front arm and back arm), and Valery Borzov #4-11 and 4-17 (back arm).

When an athlete is running at top speed or near top speed, it is critical that the back arm clears a point well behind the hip (see photo, John Carlos #3-9). To best utilize a blocking action for the development of impulse, the back arm should not completely extend at the elbow. It is best to remain 90°-100°; however, some individuals require more elbow extension because of an unusually long stride length. Regardless of the angle, the rearward arm should be stopped immediately to assure transference of force.

Leg Action and Foot Placement

For years coaches have been arguing about the proper foot placement of runners. Experts have expressed varied opinions, usually arising from a different style expressed by champion athletes. The common and often misleading styles include: sprinters should land high on the toes; distance and middle distance runners should have a ball, heel toe action, etc.

In understanding foot placement, the key is not how high or low the athlete lands upon the foot, but rather, what the mechanics of smooth running employ at various speeds of running. Foot placement teaching can be forgotten if the athlete utilizes proper motion of the legs.

Leg action should resemble circular motion, one of reciprocal innervation—the same circular constant motion we would expect to see in an efficient working machine.

In discussing foot placement, we are naturally led to comparing the distance runner and the sprinter. Primarily, the main difference in the two extreme skills is that the sprinter has a short reaction and great driving power. The distance runner on the other hand, is striving for economy of effort. Heel contact differs slightly between the distance runner and the sprinter (see photos of John Carlos and Jim Ryun). But in any type of running the heel touches the ground, and for an instant (depending upon the runner's speed) bears full weight of the body as the center of mass is positioned for the next stride.

Many involved in running are overly concerned with the emphasis needed for running on the toes by the hurdlers and sprinters. It is true that while running on the toes, the athlete becomes taller, thus increasing stride length and perhaps speed. However, it must be remembered that a *normal* efficient stride allows full foot contact with the ground regardless of the event or the speed at which the athlete is running. In addition to providing balance, a slight heel landing will enable a more forceful plantar flexion (a muscle on stretch will contract with greater force). In analyzing high speed photography of a sprinter or hurdler, it is easy to see the full foot, including the heel, in contact with the ground (see John Carlos photos #3-13 and #3-14).

The mechanical efficiency of a runner, at best, is difficult to observe due to the speed of movement and because of the many individual body differences. Ideally, however, we would expect to find several effective characteristics in proper running form. At the instant the full foot (not the heel or toes) strikes the ground, there should be somewhat of a straight line extending through the head, shoulders, hips and foot. This line will not include the knee joint as it is absorbing the force of the foot strike (see Jim Ryun #3-9 and John Carlos #3-15). Perhaps one of the worst faults of a young runner while attempting to increase stride length is reaching out with the foreleg prior to the time the foot strikes the ground. In essence, what happens is the foot lands well ahead of the knee. Each time the foot, especially the heel, strikes ahead of the knee, the athlete is applying "brakes" to momentum. It will certainly cause unnecessary soreness and perhaps injury to the knee or hips.

Of equal concern to the mechanics of running should be hip placement during the running stride. If the buttocks protrude (lordosis) causing a hollow back position, the athlete is upsetting efficiency and the ability of the body to protect itself from injury. The back normally is made up of several S-shaped curves which serve to absorb the force created by weight bearing and locomotion. To allow the whole spine to perform its job, the hips must be tucked forward. If not, all of the weight and forces center on a small area near the lumbar and sacral joint. An improper position of the hips will certainly cause pain and eventual injury. It should be remembered also that the tucked hip position will lengthen the stride considerably thus adding to the effectiveness of the runner.

Characteristics of Efficient Running and Body Displacement

The stride pattern in running consists of three distinct phases:
1. the power phase (when the rear foot pushes the athlete forward);
2. the float phase (when the runner is actually off the ground) and
3. the pulling phase (when the front has contacted the ground and begins pulling its way back).

A runner's efficiency can, in some respects, be compared to the rolling of a wheel. However, in analogy, the reader must understand that a runner moves over the ground in what kinesiologists call reciprocal motion (see Fig. 3-2). The wheel, on the other hand, is considered rotation motion. Reciprocating motion means repeated movement. The

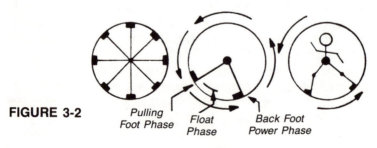

FIGURE 3-2   Pulling Foot Phase   Float Phase   Back Foot Power Phase

use of the term is ordinarily limited to movements like the bouncing of a ball or the repeated blows of a hammer, but technically can include almost all kinds of motion. The term oscillation refers to repeated angular movements such as movements in an arc—a walking or running motion.

As the wheel turns, notice that with smooth movement for the spoke (foot) to strike the ground only when it is directly under the axle (center of gravity for hips). This is the important aspect of running, i.e. striking the ground only when the hips or weight concentration are directly over the foot.

If, in the case of the wheel, the spoke contacted the ground before it was underneath the center of gravity, the spoke would necessarily be too long. On the other hand, if the spoke touched the ground only after the center of gravity was already beyond the perpendicular point, the spoke would be too short. Either the long or short spoke would greatly upset the smooth turning of the wheel. The smooth action of a runner, is affected similarly. A runner, whose foot contacts the ground well ahead of the knee of center point, breaks momentum and jars the body badly. A trait not nearly so common would be the individual whose foot strikes the ground behind the center of gravity, forcing himself to fall forward too quickly. The outcome of this action is very similar to the runner who carries the upper body forward. Both of the foregoing tendencies create vertical displacement and upset the necessary smooth, horizontal and balanced movement. (Fig. 3-3)

Hill Running

Distance runners, and many times sprinters and hurdlers, are faced with additional problems when training or competing over rough or uneven terrain. We have discussed the problems of balance, center of gravity and ultimately proper posture in running. When the runner attempts to run in the hills, all of the foregoing characteristics are disrupted due to the grade of the terrain. These disruptions must be counteracted for even a moderate amount of running efficiency under different and new circumstances.

Usually, over long periods of time in "adverse" running conditions, one can naturally adapt. However, the novice can use advice which saves valuable training time and perhaps prevents unnecessary soreness or injury which too often is the outcome of improper hill running.

The most important adaptation to hill running (either up or down) is the simple rule of thumb, "shorten the stride"! Emphasis on a shorter stride enables the athlete to keep control and adapt to the irregular braking and rotations caused by running in the hills.

FIGURE 3-3

Figure A   Figure B

FIGURE A

FIGURE B

Figure A—The Efficient "Upright" Runner: This runner has proper positioned pelvis which is the key to good posture in running. It is characterized by a flat back, upright chest and a low-on-the-foot landing. This posture reduces discomfort and possible injury. In addition it allows efficiency by allowing the body to be pushed forward by reducing vertical body displacement.

Figure B—The Inefficient "Chest Forward" Runner: The "chest forward" runner's pelvis is tipped forward. This causes several problems: all body weight falls directly upon the posterior low back area. It tends to place much weight upon the foot when landing thus absorbing momentum rather than transferring it. It does not allow full flexion of the hips and low spine extensions, thus reducing full leg action.

More specifically, what are some of the problems a runner experiences while running over rough or uneven ground? Hill running upsets the established center of gravity placement. While running uphill, the runner must assume a forward lean—due to acceleration actions—coming from the hips and ankles, or find himself bouncing up and down rather than putting power into the upgrade. At the same time, the knees must be lifted high while keeping the stride short. You may say this creates a problem as it has been pointed out that high leg lift increases stride length. This is not true when running up hills. Because of the incline, the foot strikes the ground sooner than would be the case on flat ground (see Fig. 3-4).

FIGURE 3-4

Normal Posture
Flat Running

Adjustment to Uphill Running — forward lean, high knee lift, but shortened stride.

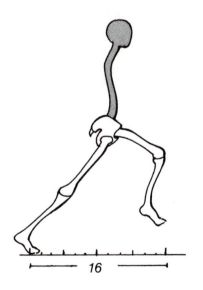

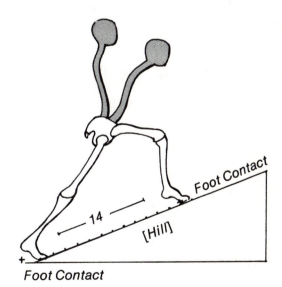

16

14   [Hill]

Foot Contact

Foot Contact

In addition, the arms and shoulders must be dropped somewhat to give less emphasis on vertical displacement. This characteristic, the arm shift, usually occurs naturally but should be practiced. The uphill runner must begin a very vigorous pumping action that is parallel to the direction of travel. Basically, a runner beginning an uphill ascent must change himself from a distance runner to a sprinter with one exception—he is not trying to increase body speed, but rather keep it constant.

Downhill running presents some of the same balance problems but in reverse. Gravity and speed tend to cause over-striding, jarring-heel landings, bouncing, loss of composure of the upper body, and flailing of the arms. The objective of running down the hills is to maintain the runner's stride flow with little or no disruption of posture, foot placement, upper body carriage and arm carriage.

While running uphill, the athlete concentrates on the high knee lift. Downhill running calls for the opposite—little or no leg lift in the front— the concern is now focused on the back kick. The body needs to be as close to the ground as possible with the foot landing lightly upon the heel.

There seems to be one characteristic which solves most of the major problems of running downhill. It indeed enhances the smooth flowing and constant stride that a runner wishes to have both for comfort and efficiency. This characteristic has to do with the height of the back kick or "kick up" toward the buttocks of the trailing leg (see Fig. 3-5). We know that normally the faster the running speed, the greater the tendency for the free foot to swing up (rotary momentum) toward the hips. This characteristic is always true in all running. The jogger has virtually no kick-up, whereas the sprinter's foot, in full speed, moves up to the hips in free-leg swing.

FIGURE 3-5

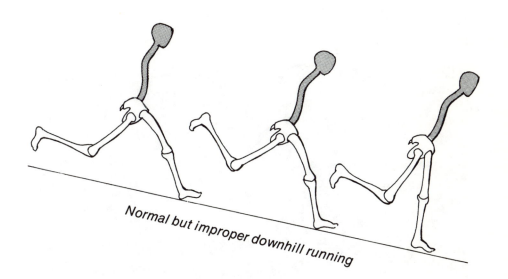

Normal but improper downhill running

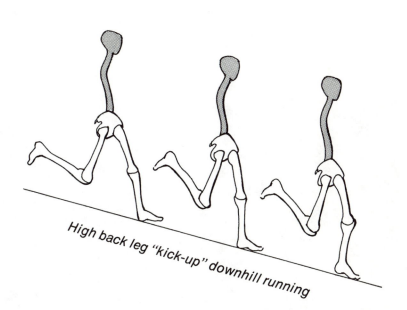

High back leg "kick-up" downhill running

JIM RYUN, U.S.A.

3-1　　　　　　　　　3-2　　　　　　　　　3-3

3-7　　　　　　　　　3-8　　　　　　　　　3-9

3-4   3-5   3-6

3-10   3-11   3-12

JOHN CARLOS, U.S.A.

3-1   3-2

3-6   3-7

3-3   3-4   3-5

3-8   3-9

3-10   3-11

3-14   3-15   3-16

3-12   3-13

3-17   3-18

4

Training for Speed in Running

Concerns For The Sprinter

Too many times we think of sprinters as being born, not developed. The biggest enjoyment I have had during coaching has been in watching an average printer substantially lower his time through intelligent work.

Several considerations must highlight an approach to sprint training. From what I have observed, simple aspects are often forgotten by coaches in preparing their athletes in both the technique of sprinting and efficient exchanges in the sprinting relays.

Quickness and stride frequency alone will not guarantee a great sprinter. We also understand that a long stride is important in gaining speed in running. However, a giant stride alone will not prepare the athlete for a record time. But by placing the two ingredients together, we have the makings for an effective sprinter.

An additional factor, that of power development, will unite the stride frequency and the long stride. So the objectives of training a sprinter become:
- increase the stride length
- frequency of stride (leg speed)
- power or impulse (force X time)

Experience has demonstrated that stride length and frequency can very well be improved upon with repetition training by the athlete. Drills are easily incorporated into the warm-up activity that preceeds each day's training session. Warm-up sprint drills not only change body temperature, increase flexibility, provide the stair case phenomena (utilize more muscle fibers and nerves through the "all or none principle"), but these drills also help develop the reflex learning patterns necessary for retention and behavioral changes.

The principle which must be remembered is simply that of specificity. To become faster, a runner must train at high speeds. That does not mean only to run as fast as possible, but to develop reflex motor nerves through speed quickness training. A runner must overload all systems which determine speed changes.

General Considerations Applied Through Research

Research is generally either ignored by a coach or abused by not applying the information. However, research does provide athletes and coaches the tools for effective training. The key is to simplify and apply the information into an everyday training situation.

Reaction Time
Reaction time is both inherited and improvable. A great sprinter can have relatively slow reaction time and a poor sprinter can have great reaction time. Reaction time is defined simply as the time from stimulus to response. The average world class sprinter has a reaction time of around .1 second. Armin Hary, the great German Olympic Gold medal winner was claimed to have a reaction time of .07 and Valery Borzov, the Russian champion, was around .1. It is interesting, indeed, that there is no real information available on the great American sprinters. To date American coaches have not taken the time nor the effort to calculate a scientific approach to developing sprinters. Instead, they are more concerned in recruiting "horses" and turning them loose on the track. The U.S.A. without doubt has the capabilities of dominating the sprint scene completely if more concern is given to development.

Reaction time, as was stated, is improvable. Improvement comes from repeated drills and working on response to a variety of stimuli to the nervous system.

Acceleration Time
Acceleration time is the mean time taken for a runner to go from a standstill to maximum speed. Interestingly, humans can accelerate for approximately 6 seconds. In fact, an inferior or young runner will reach maximum acceleration much sooner than 6 seconds. Examples of expected acceleration time from various levels of runners would include:

9.0 sprinters (100 yards) reaches maximum speed in 60.6 yards; a 9.5 sprinter reaches maximum speed in 57 yards and a 10.5 athlete reaches top speed in 53.7 yards.

Acceleration time gives the coach guidelines in establishing objectives when training sprinters, hurdlers and jumpers. For instance: sheer sprint training need not exceed 60 yards; the development of speed maintenance must be done in excess of 70-80 yards; also it has implications for changes in body lean and momentum. Body lean should occur only until maximum speed is reached. An additional area where knowledge of acceleration can really be used to an advantage is in placement of relay personnel in acceleration zones and also in the length of run-up in all jump and vault events.

Velocity Maintenance Time

Velocity maintenance time is also an important factor to a coach. This factor simply indicates that once top speed has been reached it is impossible to maintain steady velocity for more than 10-20 meters. At this point of the race, a runner *will slow down.*

The runner capable of winning a race where everything is equal to the acceleration point will be the athlete who slows down the least. Velocity maintenance probably comes from the ability to relax and from well-developed anaerobic capacity. Neuronal fatigue expressed by maintaining stride length is the most observable characteristic of the athlete losing momentum in a sprint event.

Finish Time

The final ingredient necessary to understand is finish time. We know an athlete can gain a small fraction of time by using a pronounced lean or dip at the finish line. Judge's position and photo time places are determined by the torso position as it crosses the finish line. Certainly it is possible to drop the torso ahead of the waist and legs at the finish. Timing of this skill must be incorporated into practice sessions; if this technique is performed improperly or too soon, a forward lean will cause the loss of the race or a fall. Biomechanic principles of establishing a secondary rotation (windmilling the arms) will prevent falling.

Selected Areas Of Training To Develop The Necessary Skills In Sprinting
Stride Length and Flexibility
  a. High leg running drill (warm-up)
  b. High kick drill (warm-up)
  c. Butt kick drill
  d. Hurdles—both lead legs
  e. Stadium stair sprints
  f.   Hill strides

Stride Frequency
a. Fast arm leg drill (warm-up)
b. Towing at faster than possible running speed
c. Downhill running
d. All relaxation and posture drills
e. Fast sprint drill with high knee and short stride

Power and Impulse
*a. Eccentric weight training
*b. Concentric weight training
*c. Plyometric or elastic training, including all hopping, bounding and jump work
d. Harness and belt running
e. Hill and stadium stair running
f. Arm action emphasis (to aid opposite and equal reaction)

*See section on Strength Training (plyometric)Hill strides

The Sprint Start

An economical start obviously is very important in running the short sprints. The applied mechanics of such a start should be understood both by the coach and athlete. Efficient starts are developed through a good understanding of mechanical skills, strength, joint angles, balance and weight distribution. The good start is simple and easy to learn for any athlete. However, after learning the technique, the athlete must practice the skills over and over again so as to develop a reflex response.

Evidence presented by Henry in the 1950's about force characteristics of block settings and foot placement in the starting blocks is still applicable. Of this evidence, the most important for the athlete to understand is that the feet exert nearly equal pressure during block clearance. The rear foot exerts the most force, but the front foot holds the force for a much longer period of time.

Block Settings

With a medium setting (blocks approximately 21" apart) the front foot builds to nearly 196 pounds in .5 seconds and the rear foot builds to 208 pounds in .16 seconds. This, of course, is for a mature 170-180 lb. male sprinter. In the case of a bunch start (blocks set approximately 11" apart) much less foot force on the front block can be applied due to the short period the foot is in contact with the block. Block clearance in the bunch start is indeed much faster but may be up to 12% less powerful. Therefore, a sprinter using a bunch start gets away faster but loses advantage very quickly. Pounds of pressure for the bunch start are considerably less for both feet in the narrow setting position.

The final block setting, the elongated (approximately 26" spacing), is by far the most powerful in terms of pressure exerted and also gives much more velocity during movement; but because of less dynamic strength in the average athlete, velocity cannot be maintained. In the future, as athletes become stronger they will be able to increase the width of block setting.

Perhaps the most crucial key to an effective start from blocks is the angle of the rear leg, to a lesser extent, the angle of the front leg during the set position.*

As we observe during leg pressing or squatting exercises, the most powerful position (leg angle at knee) is between 120° and 140°. Therefore, we seek a relatively straight back leg when starting. It should, however, never be completely extended, for to get any movement it must bend before it can extend. The front leg should approximate 90° and the two legs should provide force as equal as possible.

The following provides a check list for taking the marks, getting set and action at the time of the gun.

Check List For Setting Blocks:

1. The front block is set so the knee touches the starting line when lowered.
2. The distance between the blocks is determined by the angle of the leg and the size of the athlete.
3. The front leg should be bent in a 90° angle at the knee when in the set position. This foot applies force for a long period and begins in a weak position but gradually changes to a strength and power position.
4. The rear leg should be bent in a 120°-140° angle at the knee in the set position. It exerts the major portion of power immediately.
5. Check to see that lower legs are near parallel. This gives a summation of force delivered from both legs.

Head and Eyes

1. Head in direct line with the body.
2. Eye focus should be directed at the spot where the first foot strikes the ground after the start.
3. After the start, do not raise the head quickly, as it will lower the hips and shorten the strides.

To Your Marks

1. Back into the blocks; never allow yourself to compress prior to taking your mark. Stay loose and stretch as long as possible. Don't hurry but do not delay.

---

*Henry, Franklin, "Research on Spring Running," **The Athletic Journal,** 1952.

2. Position the rear leg with toes barely touching the ground and leg straight.
3. Position the front leg with toes barely touching the ground and leg straight.
4. Place one hand at a time. Form a good base (triangle) with the fingers.
5. Hunch the back. Make the shoulders high (from the ground).
6. Shift the weight forward so the shoulders are in front of the starting line and your hand.
7. The arms should support the major portion of body weight.

FIGURE 4-1
Basic Set Position

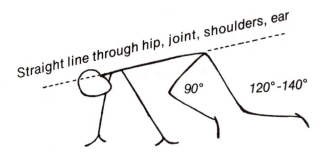

Basic Set Position

One of the primary objectives of a sprint start is to place the center of gravity on as close a plane as possible as the upright athlete running full speed. When the athlete is in the "set position," all possible means to raise the center of gravity should be employed. Body stance to accomplish a maximal height for center of gravity should be:

- High on finger tips.
- Toes barely touching the ground in block.
- Upper back and shoulder held as high as possible.
- Elbows completely extended.
- Feet straight in the blocks.

Hip Position

The elevation of the hips (higher than level of shoulders) is determined by drawing an imaginary line extending through the hip bones, shoulders and ears; then make a determination of the angle represented at the knee of the back leg. If the hip point rises during the start, the hips are too low in the set position; if the hip point drops during the start, the hips were too high. Note that moving the hip height will change the angle of the legs.

Action At The Gun
1. Arm and leg movement:
    a. The initial movement is to pick up and drive the left arm (left foot forward) with no across-chest movement. The right comes back with a 90° flexion of the elbow.
    b. Right leg and left leg should begin immediate extension.
2. Head and eye focus will come up with the body. A major mistake of many sprinters is to lift the head and eyes immediately as the gun sounds; this causes the hips to drop and a shorter than desirable step to develop.
3. Body lean is determined by the amount of acceleration. When acceleration ceases, there must be no deviation from a vertical position.
4. Watch for "looping" of the rear leg—it must be brought forward in as low a position as possible. Remember, the shortest distance between the blocks and the next step is a straight line.
5. Emphasis must be on relaxation of the arms and face—but arm thrust is important in providing impulse.
6. Develop a routine and be prepared to react to proper commands.

Training to Develop the Start
1. The lunge belt
2. Hill sprints
3. Weight training
4. Arm development through arm action drills
    a. Reaction type
    b. Endurance type
5. Starts
    a. With proper commands and gun
    b. With competition
6. The warm-up
    (Tests have shown that the 8th to the 12th start is the fastest.)

Coaching Tips
1. Watch initial arm action off the line. Lead arm should be parallel to the ground, back arm should come up hard behind but never extend at elbow.
2. Check hip height.
3. Check angle of the legs in the set position.
4. Check block settings from line to front foot and between feet.

5. Check hand and finger placement.
6. Weight should be forward.
7. Check to see that on command "set" there is no further forward motion.
8. Check to see if forward knee is under body and between elbows.
9. Stress reaction to the gun. Use different signals.
10. Check head and remind runner about eye focus.
11. Tests have shown that the 8th-12th start in sequence is fastest.

Suggested Relay Techniques

4 X 100 Sprint Relay

Number One Man: Lines up angled from the outside in and run as close to the curb as possible. He is to carry the baton with the extreme end in his right hand.

Number Two Man: Lines up in a three or four point stance on the outside of his lane approximately 10 meters behind the Olympic 30-meter extension zone. He is to look back either over his inside shoulder or between his legs. Through long practice with the incoming man, he will determine a *lean* and *go* mark. Normally, the lean mark is approximately 10-12 meters out and the go mark 6-7 meters back. He is to *take-off in a normal sprint start fashion.* When the incoming runner yells a command, the left arm will be straight back with the palm up. The arm should never have to be extended during more than 1 and ½ steps. This arm should be near shoulder height. It is the outgoing man's responsibility to pull the baton away from the incoming runner.

Number Three Man: With the exception that he lines up on the inside of his lane and is to take the baton in the right hand, the process is the same.

Number Four Man: Lives up on the outside of his lane and takes the baton with his left hand.

In all of the above exchanges, the baton does a series of flip flops during the race. The outgoing runner will always receive an extended half of the baton, and there should never be a need to adjust the baton for more "handle."

4 X 400 Relay

It has been estimated that an average of two seconds can be made up on a visual pass by proper execution of the baton exchange and by not changing hands with the baton.

Remember, it takes 60 yards to approach full speed. You never allow the receiver to assume the speed of the passer. The receiver accelerates through the zone. It is much more efficient to allow the incoming man to get close and sprint out than it is for the outgoing man to move slowly assuming incoming man's speed.

We prefer to "look in" and receive baton with left hand, as this can protect us somewhat. Also, we don't want a cross over of the baton.

Number One Man: Begins with baton in right hand.

Number Two Man: Stands on outside of lane, judges distance and sprints out for three steps, turns, and receives baton with left hand (palm up, looking between "V" formed by thumb and index finger).

Number Three Man: Stands inside and looks out, incoming runner runs to outside of lane, outgoing man takes baton with right hand.

Number Four Man: Is the same as the number two man. The exchange zone and corner are "Key Areas." It is very difficult to pass an opponent in zone or on corner. Run first 110 yards with speed and authority.

Some Concerns In Running The Short Relay

Yard-for-yard, number 1 and 3 runners will spend more time influencing baton speed because of the retarding effects of the turn as curve. This will amount to 0.3 seconds or more.

It is extremely important for each incoming runner to carry the baton through nearly all the acceleration phase and passing zone (30 meters).

Yearly Training Four Phase Emphasis Progression For Short Sprints and High Hurdles

(These dates are approximated and must be dictated by weather and schedule)

The following program is adapted from Gerard Mach's Polish Sprint Training Program. It is, however, adapted to meet the school and competition track programs at most high schools and colleges.

PHASE #1
Sept.-Oct.-Nov.
Major emphasis of cycle=70%
cycle=70-80%

    a. general endurance 10%
    b. strength endurance 20%
    c. tempo endurance 25%
    d. special endurance 10%
    e. stride length and flexibility 5%

PHASE #3
March-April
Major emphasis of

    a. power speed 15%
    b. special endurance 20%
    c. stride frequency 10%
    d. impulse 15%
    e. speed 20%

Minor emphasis=30%
- a. power speed
- b. speed
- c. technique

PHASE #2
Dec.-Jan.-Feb.
Major emphasis of cycle=70%
- a. power speed 10%
- b. special endurance 20%
- c. strength endurance 20%
- d. tempo endurance 10%
- e. stride length 5%
- f. stride frequence 5%

Minor emphasis=30%
- a. special endurance 10%
- b. general endurance 10%
- c. speed 10%

Minor emphasis=20-30%
- a. stride length 10%
- b. strength endurance 20%
- c. general endurance 5%
- d. tempo endurance 5%

PHASE #4
May-June
Major emphasis of cycle=80-85%
- a. speed and skill 30%
- b. power speed 10-20%
- c. stride frequency 20%
- D. impulse 10-15%

Minor emphasis=15-20%
- a. special endurance 5%
- b. endurance 5%
- c. strength endurance 5%

Yearly Training Four Phase Emphasis Progression For Long Sprint And Intermediate Hurdles

(The dates are approximated and dictated by weather and meet schedule)

PHASE #1
Sept.-Oct.-Nov.
Major emphasis of cycle=70%
- a. general endurance 10%
- b. strength endurance 20%
- c. temp 25%
- d. special endurance 10%
- e. stride length and flexibility 5%

Minor emphasis=30%
- a. power speed 15%
- b. speed and technique 15%

PHASE #3
March-April
Major emphasis of cycle=70-80%
- a. power speed 20%
- b. impulse 20%
- c. special endurance 20%
- d. strength endurance 10%
- e. speed 10%

Minor emphasis=20-30%
- a. stride length 5%
- b. stride frequency 10%
- c. general endurance 10%

PHASE #2
Dec.-Jan.-Feb.
Major emphasis of cycle=80%
  a. power speed 20%
  b. impulse 20%
  c. strength endurance 20%
  d. tempo endurance 20%

Minor emphasis=30%
  a. special endurance 10%
  b. general endurance 10%
  c. speed 10%

PHASE #4
May-June
Major emphasis of cycle=80-85%
  a. speed and skill 20%
  b. power speed 20%
  c. impulse 20%
  d. special endurance 10%
  e. stride frequency 10-15%

Minor emphasis=15-20%
  a. general endurance 10%
  b. strength endurance 10%

Keys To Percentage Charts Listed Above

I Stride Length And Flexibility
  a. High leg drill
  b. High kick-but kick
  c. Stretching
  d. Hurdles
  e. Down hill (assisted running)
  f. Tow training (assisted running)
II Stride Frequency
  a. Fast leg arm reaction drill
  b. Stadium stair and step running
  c. Towing or down hill running
  d. High leg (quick) sprint drill
III Impulse
  a. stretch acceleration running
  b. all plyometrics
  c. belt sprinting
  d. hopping and bounding
  e. arm reaction drills
IV Strength Endurance
  a. running repeats which
     exceed 10 repetitions
  b. weights which exceed 10 reps.
  c. up hill running

V Special Endurance
     (Anaerobic, 385 yds.-down)
  a. 165-220-330-358 yd.
     repeats. ⅞ to full effort, not to
     exceed 4 repetitions.
  b. steady pace 500-600
     aerobic-anerobic work
     (these workouts should not
     be run two days in a row.
VI Tempo-Endurance
  a. Pace awareness in
     interval work
  b. Early season, more workload
     with short recovery
  c. Late season, less workload
     with more recovery.
VII SPEED TRAINING
  a. 30-80 yards standing or
     running start.
  b. all sprint drills
  c. stadium stair sprinting
  d. all block work-with or
     without the belt
  e. plyometrics
  f. all reaction work
  g. finish dip at tape

Valery Borsov's Start

During Valery Borsov's international sprint supremacy one could not help but see a unique starting technique much in contrast to the accepted techniques of other world class sprinters. There has been considerable speculation and much analysis as to the effectiveness of his start. However, many of the techniques he used still remain a mystery.

The major differences between his block position and others are:

1. Head and eye contact is down between the hands; this takes some of the alignment away from the head and shoulders.
2. The center of mass is located directly between (midway) feet and hands. Other sprinters center the weight more on the hands.
3. Hip height is elevated 10-12 inches above the shoulder.
4. Front leg angle is closer to 100° than our standard 90.°
5. Block spacing is a "bunch" (feet approximately 8"-10" apart). This provides almost parallel force in the drive from both legs.
6. Front foot is in contact with the ground *and* the block pedal. The assumption here is that allowing more foot contact yields more muscle summation as the instant stretch reflexes are initiated.

WEEKLY WORKOUT SAMPLE
for
Sprinters - Quarter Milers - Hurdlers

NAME: Sprinters   **DATE:** Dec. 1, 1983

1. **Easy jog**	23. **Finish line drills** a. From 50 yds. b. From 30 yds. c. From 20 yds. d. From last hurdle e. From full trial distance
2. **50 yds. high & fast leg drill**	
3. **70 yds. of stretch accelerations**	24. **Spring drill**
4. **Drills** a. b. c.	
5. **Belts**	M (1 Around Park) (Stretching)(2×8 to 40) (9a RR-LL to 40×8) (24×6 to 40) (10g ×4 ¾ speed - Continuous Running) (full weights)
6. **Stadium stair sprinting**	
7. **Hill work** a. protest (1) up (2) down b. Ann Morrison (1) up (2) down c. Americana (1) up (2) down	Tu (1 Around foot bridge) (stretching) (2×8 to 40) (14×4 with belts, 14×5 Medium Speed) (24 × 6 to 40) (2 mile run along river)
8. **Hurdles** a. High b. Intermediate c. Low	W (1 to 2 miles) (Stretching) (2×8 to 40) (24 ×4 to 40)(13c ×6) (10 K ×4 drop down - start at 44 (full weights)
9. **Plyometrics** a. Slow hopping, single leg to 50 yds. b. Fast hopping, both legs to 50 yds. c. Hopping onto & off box d. Lateral box jumping e. Double leg take-off	

92

10. Sets a. 40   b. 50   c. 60   d. 70   e. 80   f. 100
g. 110   h. 165   i. 180   j. 220   k. 330   l. 352
m. 440   n. 500   o. 550   p. 600   q. 660   r. 880
s. 1000

11. Dropdowns (same letters as above)
Running start (same letters as above)
Running start drills
a. From 20 yds–20 yds.
b. From 20 yds–30 yds.
c. From 20 yds–40 yds.
d. From 20 yds–50 yds.

14. Starts (same letters as #10)

15. Relay exchanges
a. Hand drills   b. Timed exchanges
c. ¾ effort   d. Continuous
e. Various leg timing drills

16. Distance run

17. Individual therapy or rehabilitation

18. Indian running

19. Meet with coach   a. Film study   b. Pictures

20. Pool   a. swimming   b. running intervals in deep
water   c. running interals in shallow water

21. Workout of your choice

22. Weights   a. General   b. Circuit   c. Power sets

Th (Run 5 continuous miles)
Stretch x 10 –15 minutes

F (1 to 1 mile to Protest – Stretch x 10 min)
(7a x 8 – Run 4 Steady & 4 Drop Down)
(Easy Running back to Gym)
(9a x 6 ea. leg indoor) (24x4) (stretch again)

Sa Long Easy Running
on your own,
Stretch

Su

Stretch

Comments:

93

4-4   4-3

4-8   4-7

VALERIY BORZOV, U.S.S.R.

4-2   4-1

4-6   4-5

4-12   4-11

4-18   4-17   4-16

4-10   4-9

4-15   4-14   4-13

5

Developing Speed in Hurdling

Good performance in hurdling calls for more than mechanical perfection. It demands speed as well. A time study indicates the event is little more than a sprint event over ten obstacles. In a championship race of 110 meters, only 1.8-2.0 seconds are expended in clearing the hurdles. This breaks down to less than .2 seconds per hurdle. The rest of the time is occupied in sprinting.

Thus, all manipulations going into and coming off the hurdle must be designed to maintain linear momentum at the maximum rate of speed. The task of the hurdler is to race the course with good sprint technique, deviating as little as possible over the barriers. Form is important, of course, but the hurdler should not become obsessed with it. The accent must be on getting to the tape as quickly as possible.

As in all events discussed, the particular problem of hurdling simply centers around effective placement of the center of gravity over the hurdle, regardless of the type (highs, intermediates, womens or lows). The hurdle must be negotiated with as little variance as possible of the center of gravity.

Body position changes greatly affect the position of the gravity center or weight displacement. (Fig. 5-1)

FIGURE 5-1
Examples of Changes in Center of Mass as Body Positions Change

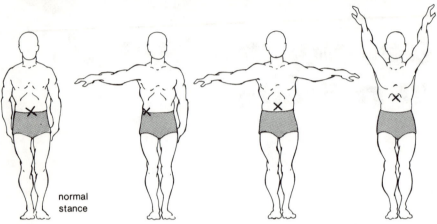

normal
stance

The High Hurdles

The Start And Approach To The First Hurdle

The hurdle start differs from the regular sprint start technique in perhaps two major aspects. First, the hurdler must drive up and out rather than out and up. In fact the good hurdler usually achieves full-sprinting position in approximately 4 yards, thus enabling him to concentrate on the proper hurdle clearance. The sprinter, on the other hand, may require up to 15 yards to achieve the desired upright position.

The second point of difference lies in the fact that the hurdler must predetermine a spot for his take-off.

Hurdlers use a varied number of steps to the first barrier. The optimum varies from seven to nine, with eight apparently furnishing the best results for the average-sized athlete. The desired rate is a series of *full power* strides. The athlete who cannot achieve such uniformity will find himself chopping or overstretching in order to reach the scheduled take-off point. The result is a loss of momentum.

As a rule, the athlete will take-off from a point about 7'6" from the hurdle, the precise distance depending upon running speed, leg length, and lead leg speed. Since it takes approximately 40-60 yards to achieve full speed, the take-off distance for the first hurdle will be slightly less than the take-off distance for that of the succeeding hurdles. (This is to compensate for the lesser speed.)

When fatigue sets in toward the end of the race, the take-off distance is again slightly shortened because of diminished running speed.

The beginning athlete, in his eagerness to generate speed, tends to overemphasize his normal stride. This not only makes for inefficient sprinting, but tends to bring the athlete too close to the hurdles.

In his speed training, the hurdler must learn to emphasize a vigorous, short arm cycle rather than a long, stroking arm action. The latter tends to level out the running stride and thus destroy the essential high knee action. It also forces the runner back on the heels when the weight should be forward.

The final point to remember in the approach is the last stride must be slightly shorter than the previous two or three strides. This will allow the athlete to position the center of gravity correctly and leave the ground with a forward thrust of the trunk. The objective in hurdle clearance is a long, gradual horizontal arc rather than a short vertical curve which will destroy momentum.

As a beginning athlete comes off the hurdle, the action is usually one of a short stride with the trailing leg, immediately followed by a longer stride. Through practice, the hurdler should achieve a three-step pattern (between hurdles) in which the first two steps are even, but slightly longer than the third. The shorter last step will allow the center of gravity to pass forward over the ball of the foot, facilitating a vigorous dive or "buck" with the upper body.

This short step pattern also tends to make the flight pattern flat and horizontal rather than circular and vertical. Even the smallest degree of circular motion increases the distance of the center of gravity from the take-off and touch down points, costing the athlete valuable hundredths of seconds.

Mechanics Over The Hurdle

Since no real power can be developed in the air, the dive or "buck" must be initiated on the ground prior to the take-off. For this reason, teaching trunk thrust and low horizontal positioning must begin with the lead leg as it goes into the hurdle. It should be remembered that maximal power cannot be exerted from a flat foot, on the heel, running position. The hurdler must run as high on the toes as possible because:

- It makes the individual taller, thus reducing the need to raise the center of gravity while passing over the hurdle.
- It permits a full application of force originating from the larger muscles of the leg and ending in the toes.
- It places the athlete in position for essential trunk thrust.

The importance of running high on the toes has been emphasized by many coaches. It has been claimed that the athlete who lands and takes off from the heels will waste approximately .1 per each ten yards, thus losing a full second over a 110 meter race. (Fig. 5-2)

FIGURE 5-2

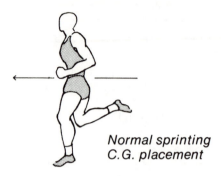

*Normal sprinting
C.G. placement*

FIGURE 5-3

Inefficient

*High center of gravity
and parabola*

More Efficient

*Low center of gravity
and flat parabola*

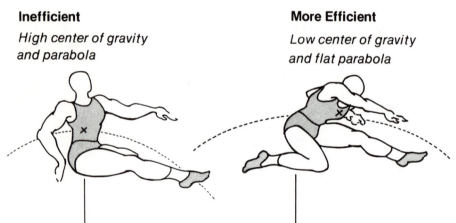

*Effective hurdling means keeping center of gravity constant both
horizontally and vertically.*

Take-Off Point

Insofar as the take-off point is concerned, we again advocate a distance of from seven to eight feet from the barrier. The height and speed of the athlete are the important factors in determining this distance. For example, the shorter athlete must take-off farther out from the hurdle, as he must raise his center of gravity more than would the taller athlete.

The athlete's speed is also a factor. The faster the speed, the farther out the take-off and landing points. This is necessary in increasing the horizontal plane and reducing the circular or vertical path component.

The lead leg now becomes a factor in controlling the flight path over the hurdle; the closer the athlete is able to get down is a direct result of the lead leg speed. The slower the lead leg comes up, the farther back the take-off point must be and the greater the danger of getting the center of gravity too high.

The lead leg should move into position while flexed at the knee (see Willie Davenport photos 5-8, 5-9, 5-10). The reason for this is: first, a straight lead leg forces the upper body back and out of the ideal sprint lean required for maximal speed; second, a completely extended leg tends to force a rotation of the leg over the side of the hurdle, which will throw the entire body out of alignment.

As the lead leg moves toward the hurdle, the athlete should begin to thrust the upper body and arms toward the barrier (See Davenport photos 5-11, 5-12, 5-13, 5-14). I call this explosive movement the dive or "buck." It is indeed helpful for the athlete to drop the head at the instant the upper body moves forward and down. The weight of the head and the chest was creating a lifting effect on the lead leg (Newton's Third Law). A proper "buck" will place or nearly place the hurdler's chest on the thigh of the lead leg. If this movement is initiated too soon, the "bucking" action can cause the lead leg to hit the hurdle as the parabola will be dropping rather than rising. (Fig. 5-3) The shoulders must remain square throughout the "buck," especially when coming off the hurdle. This square shoulder movement is very difficult for the beginner to master as the arm on the same side as the leading leg is allowed to move behind the body. This action is natural because the arm action is a reaction to the movement of the heavier leg. There are, however, ways of absorbing this rotational tendency of the upper body. For example, instruct the athlete to drive with both arms. The arm on the same side as the leading leg must stay on the hip. It must not travel behind the hips. (Davenport photos 5-15, 5-16). However, the two most important items necessary to negate unwanted rotation are: (1) The buck itself; and (2) a long (extended elbow) low pulling arm. The straighter (thus longer) the athlete is able to make this lever, the more it will counteract the weight of the heavy trailing leg.

The leading arm, when thrust over and down with the "buck," will enhance the flat horizontal flight. The athlete should not be instructed to reach for the toe, yet the thrust should be forward enough to enable the shoulders to be well down. The total action of the lead arm should be "out-down-and back." (See Davenport photos 5-15 through 5-23 - the lead and pull arm.)

Our next consideration is that of getting the lead leg down and back to the track as quickly as possible. An athlete is *unable* to get the leg back to the track by simply pushing it into the desired position. Rather, it is accomplished through the opposite and equal reaction of the lower body (leg) with that of the upper body (chest). As soon as the trailing leg crosses the hurdle it must be drawn up into the arm pit as the head and trunk are vigorously brought back to the upright running position.

103

Biomechanically, this action forces the lead leg back to the ground. Because of the established parabola, the return of the head and the upper body back to the vertical is the only maneuver the athlete can employ to get the foot down quickly.

Although emphasis is placed upon a quick trailing leg, it is important that the leg not be jerked through. It must be a fast, smooth, and continual pull. This was described graphically by "the old hurdle coach," Forest Towns. He described the knee as being attached to the leading hand by a long cord with a supporting pulley located in front of the hurdler so that a back swing of the arm would pull the leg forward. He maintained the trail leg should in effect be pulled through by the leading arm, while preparing for the next step.

If the trail leg is pulled too fast, an immediate loss of body balance will be experienced, as all the weight will drop to one side of the body. Perhaps the best way to discern the effectiveness of the trailing leg is to observe the actual hurdle clearance from the side, focusing on the relationship between the trailing knee and the hip region. In any correct hurdle clearance, the knee should cross the barrier at the same instant as the hips. If the knee is crossing prior to the hips, the athlete is lifting the leg too slowly at the take-off.

In landing, the weight (center of mass) must be over or just ahead of the weight bearing foot. (See Willie Davenport photos 5-27, 5-28.) If, the weight is too far forward, the athlete is thrown into a "braking" position, thus halting momentum. If, on the other hand the weight is too far back, the athlete will be thrown forward into a very short step. It is absolutely necessary that the trailing knee be brought through into the area of the armpit, so the first step can be long, driving and powerful.

Finishing The Race

Although the athlete will begin to tire over the last two or three hurdles, the usual advice given to him (and sprinters) is to run through the tape to a point ten yards beyond. This is unrealistic; many races, in fact, are decided by a lunge or shoulder drop into the tape. This technique is extremely valuable, though it demands precise timing. That's the reason it should be practiced almost every day. The experienced hurdler will find that the sixth stride will place him at (or just short of) the finish line. It's thus possible to perfect a shoulder drop or lunge at this number six stride.

The Intermediate Hurdles

The intermediate hurdler is usually considered a man among men and a lady among ladies when it comes to toughness and athletic ability. This individual, to excel, must be an excellent 400 runner in addition to being an excellent hurdler who can hurdle well with either lead leg. In addition, the athlete must be so conditioned that he/she can hurdle even when tired.

The intermediate hurdles are really just beginning to appear on a national level. Even though the U.S.A. has had the world's best intermediate hurdlers for several years, the prep athletes and the women on the college level are just now beginning to take the event seriously.

Perhaps the most important ingredient in running the 400 hurdles is to develop a stride pattern which falls directly into the space between the individual barriers. This is important, not only because it gives better speed but also because it allows the athlete to conserve energy, necessary even to finishing a race let alone perform well.

Characteristics of the Intermediate Hurdles

Athletes who attempt to run the 400 hurdles usually do not understand or practice efficient hurdle clearance. There are many more rotational problems concerned with the intermediates as opposed to the highs. To compound the problem, most intermediate hurdlers are usually converted high hurdlers or sprinters. To get the necessary efficiency from hurdling technique the athlete must understand how to combat the problems of motion unique to the intermediates.

These problems are generally grouped into two areas. They are: (1) centrifugal force which will operate on all barriers located on a curve, producing interrupted speed (caused by body rotational forces coming into and off the hurdle); and (2) excessive center of gravity displacement caused by the 36" barrier as opposed to the high hurdle.

The problem of the centrifugal force which is created is much more pronounced than the onlooker would suspect. It causes a definite tendency to drift toward the outside of the lane when the athlete is in the air over the barrier. The 200 and 400 sprinters soon learn that to get around the corner efficiently they must lean into the curve and over-emphasize the outside arm action. This skill compensates somewhat for the forces that pull the body away from the inside of the lane. The hurdler, too, must make adjustments by taking a straight line lead into each barrier that is located on a curve. To counteract rotation, the hurdler must leave the ground in a linear rather than circular direction. This straight line approach cannot be developed in the air, rather it must be initiated on the ground prior to take-off.

In all circular races it is advisable to run as closely to the inside of the lane as possible. The runner who does not will increase the total distance of the race. However, in this event, the athlete needs to "drift" to the middle of the lane a couple of steps prior to the take-off. This action will in essence straighten out the curve going into and coming off from the hurdle.

It is a big advantage for the intermediate hurdler to lead with the inside (left) leg. This will give added compensation away from centrifugal force as it minimizes drifting while in the air. In addition to counteracting rotation, the left lead leg will help the athlete to clear the barrier "legally". Many times the right lead leg hurdler will not advance the trailing leg fully over the plane of the barrier; thus disqualification of the right-legged hurdler is common.

FIGURE 5-4

Drifting to the middle of the lane

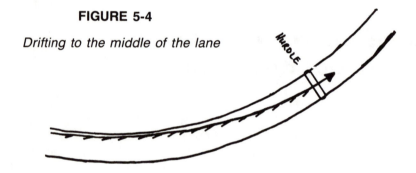

Stride Patterns to the First Hurdle

The distance from the start to the first hurdle is 45 meters or 147'9". Most intermediate hurdlers will take from 21 to 23 strides to the first barrier. When an odd number of steps are used, the right foot is back in the blocks or on the starting line.

One approach to developing a stride pattern that has good results is to place the block in the normal starting position on the line, then go out to the track to a point 7' (mark it) in front of the spot the first hurdle would be sitting. This mark represents the approximate take-off point. Forgetting the hurdle, run the athlete out of the blocks similar to running an open 400. Repeat this several times, marking the track at the spot the right foot hits closest to your original mark 7' from the hurdle's resting place. From this, set the hurdle on the track 7' from the athlete's established check mark. The hurdle will probably be closer to the starting line than its official resting place. However, with continual practice of running over the "closer" hurdle, the athlete will become more and more confident, and very gradually the hurdle can be moved toward its normal placement. This set-up works well for any hurdle race (high hurdles, etc) regardless of which number hurdle you need to establish the stride pattern.

The question is, which is best—to run with a 21 or 23 stride pattern. A younger athlete should never have to over-stride to achieve the desired number of steps, even if it means 24 strides to the first hurdle. For the experienced athlete we do have some facts. During the 1968 Olympics those athletes who used 22 strides had a faster time to the number one hurdle than those who ran with 21 strides. It is also interesting to note that a time of 5.8 to 6.1 seconds from the start to the first hurdle is necessary to be at or around world record time; 6.3 is a reasonably fast time for a college runner, 6.5 is too slow.[1]

The big concern is for athletes to reach the first barrier with an even running stride regardless of the number of steps taken.

Success with steps to the first hurdle will not be an immediate factor for the beginning athlete. It is usually wise to make gradual adjustments rather than serious alterations in block spacing (changing the forward to the back foot in the blocks) or having the athlete really stretch for that first hurdle.

The last problem of motion, excessive center of gravity displacement unique to the 30-36" barrier, is more of recognition than development. The 36" intermediate hurdle presents a somewhat more difficult technique than found in the high hurdles. This is especially true for the average-sized male athlete. The woman hurdler working over 30" usually will not need to alter technique when moving from the 100 meter hurdles to the intermediate hurdles. The man, on the other hand, needs to make some adjustments when coming from the 42" high hurdle to the lower intermediate hurdle. Usually we estimate that a high hurdler is in the air from 10-11' when running high hurdles. The intermediate hurdler will be airbourne from 12-12½ feet. This presents some problems. Too many intermediate hurdlers float this 12 foot distance (a passive action). We must recognize that any hurdler, to be effective, must maintain constant arm and leg movement. Any neglect of this active motion will cause rotation in the air and during the critical landing.

[1]**Hirschi,** Robison, Jensen, James, **Modern Techniques of Track and Field**, Lea and Febiger, Philadelphia, 1974.

Constant movement establishes a secondary axis, which prevents unwanted rotational movement. In addition, the floating or passive action will cause the hurdler to land on a "dead" foot rather than an active pawing foot. The intermediate hurdler as well as the high hurdler must achieve a sprinting action throughout the race. The difference between the intermediate and high hurdle landing is that the lead leg should not be cut down as quickly as in the highs. This generally is accomplished by a less forceful "buck" of the leading arm, head and shoulders. The intermediate hurdler needs a long-reaching action of the leading arm, but should not attempt to place the chest on the lead leg. In addition, this now leading arm must initiate the pull through of the trail leg much as it would for the high hurdler. Again, the athlete must work with an arm which is extended at the elbow. This allows a longer level.

Number of Steps Between Hurdles

The spacing between all intermediate hurdles is 35 meters or 38 yards 10 inches. The average experienced hurdler will be in the air, as mentioned, approximately 12 feet (around 7'6" from the point of take-off to the center of the hurdle and approximately 4'3" from the center of the hurdle to the landing point). This leaves approximately 34 yards to be run to reach the next hurdle. This distance with an average running stride of 6'10" requires a 15-stride approach between the hurdles; 15 steps for at least half the race is necessary for an athlete to be even an average intermediate hurdler. By dropping down to a 13-step stride approach, the average stride length increases to a little over a 7'10". This is certainly not extreme as a good sprinter's stride length is usually a little over 8'. Achieving a 13-stride approach, there-fore, is probably more a problem of confidence and coping with fatigue than physical ability for the mature male athlete.

Worthy of mention is another stride approach that has a good deal of merit for most athletes, and that is an approach of 14 strides between hurdles. When the 400 hurdler moves to the "even" number of steps, it means the lead leg will have to be alternated at each hurdle take-off.

Initially when a youngster begins setting a rhythm necessary to run the 35 meter distance, he or she would do best to establish a definite pattern with the hurdles set on the straight. If stride difficulties arise in the 15-step approach, then temporary adjustments should be made in hurdle placement. That is, the barriers should be moved closer than the official distance until a stride rhythm is established. Then gradually move the hurdle to its official distance. After confidence and strength have been developed on the straight and at the race distance, the athlete can advance to corner running.

WEEKLY WORKOUT SHEET
for Sprinters - Quarter Milers - Hurdlers
NAME: Hurdlers   **DATE:** 11/16/82

1. **Easy jog**

2. **50 yds. high & fast leg drill**

3. **70 yds. of stretch accelerations**

4. **Drills** (a)   (b)   (c)

5. **Belts**

6. **Stadium stair sprinting**

7. **Hill work**
   a. protest   (1) up   (2) down
   b. Ann Morrison   (1) up   (2) down
   c. Americana   (1) up   (2) down

8. **Hurdles**
   (a) High   (b) Intermediate   (c) Low

9. **Plyometrics**
   (a) Slow hopping, single leg to 50 yds.
   (b) Fast hopping, both legs to 50 yds.
   (c) Hopping onto & off box
   (d) Lateral box jumping
   (e) Double leg take-off

10. **Sets** (a) 40   (b) 50   (c) 60   (d) 70   (e) 80
    (f) 100   (g) 110   (h) 165   (i) 180   (j) 220
    (k) 330   (l) 352   (m) 440   (n) 500   (o) 550
    (p) 600   (q) 660   (r) 880   (s) 1000

11. **Dropdowns** (same letters as above)

12. **Running start** (same letters as above)
13. **Running start drills**
    (a) From 20 yds—20 yds.
    (b) From 20 yds—30 yds.
    (c) From 20 yds—40 yds.
    (d) From 20 yds—50 yds.

14. **Gun starts** (same letters as #10)

15. **Relay exchanges**
    (a) Hand drills   (b) Timed exchanges
    (c) ¾ effort   (d) Continuous
    (e) Various leg timing drills

16. **Distance run**

17. **Individual therapy or rehabilitation**

18. **Indian running**

19. **Meet with coach**   (a) Film study   (b) Pictures

20. **Pool**   (a) swimming   (b) running intervals in deep water   (c) running interals in shallow water

21. **Workout of your choice**

22. **Weights**   (a) General   (b) Circuit   (c) Powersets

23. **Finish line drills**
    (a) From 50 yds.
    (b) From 30 yds.
    (c) From 20 yds.
    (d) From last hurdle
    (e) From full trial distance

Th Same as Sprinters

Fr Warm-Up Running to 2 miles
5 Step Hurdle Work - to 110 Meters
Then to Weight Room - 100 Meters×5

Sa

Su

M Long Hurdlers - Run 6×22 over IH with 5 min. between.
Short Hurdlers - 6× Hurdles set close to 80 then 6×220's with Sprinters (weight Room)

Tu Same as Sprinters only over hurdles for all starts & sprints.

W

Weight:
Comments:

109

5-6 **5-5** **5-4**

5-12 **5-11** **5-10**

5-16 **5-15**

WILLIE DAVENPORT, U.S.A.

5-3   5-2   5-1

5-9   5-8   5-7

5-14   5-13

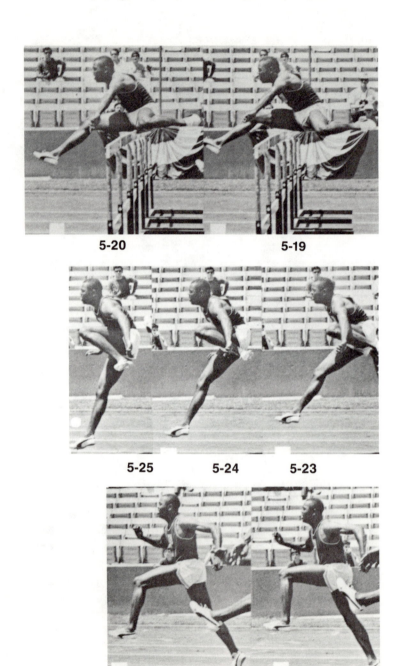

5-20   5-19

5-25   5-24   5-23

5-30   5-29

5-18   **5-17**

5-22   **5-21**

5-28   **5-27**   **5-26**

5-6   5-5

5-12   5-11   5-10

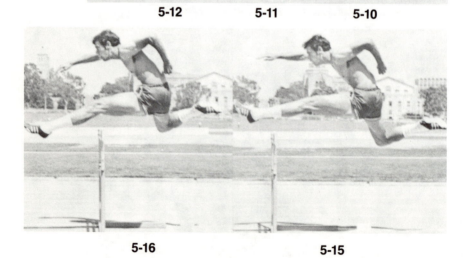

5-16   5-15

RALPH MANN

5-4 5-3 5-2 5-1

5-9 5-8 5-7

5-14 5-13

5-19   **5-18**

5-25   **5-24**   **5-23**

5-17

5-22   5-21   5-20

6

High Jump: Straddle Jumping

Straddle Jumping

Accent on the Take-Off

Many high jumpers and coaches spend so much time developing manipulations over the bar, they neglect perhaps the most important phase of the event—the initial take-off from the ground.

Geoffrey Dyson, in his excellent MECHANICS OF ATHLETICS, pointedly states that "Spring can account for approximately 90% of height obtained; this, coupled with layout, is the key factor in high jumping." Regardless of the jumping style used, certain mechanical applications are specifically geared to get the athlete off the ground by utilizing speed and lifting force.

The first consideration, however, is strength. There's absolutely no substitute for strength, especially in the lower body. This strength, developed through progressive weight training, is needed to convert speed into lift. A lack of strength at the take-off can dissipate the effect of the approach.

Secondly, consideration must be given to flexibility in the pelvis area. Flexibility produces the wide range of motion at the take-off and furnishes impetus to the rotation around the bar. The neglect of these two considerations will severely limit the jumper's ability to gain impressive heights.

Angles and Speed of Approach

Angled approaches are important to every style of jump. They permit greater freedom for the lead-leg swing and allow a portion of the body to be on the inside of the bar before the center of gravity reaches a high point.

In establishing the proper angle, the athlete should consider the two possible extremes of jumping: the 45-degree angle and the straight-on approach.

In the former, the jumper tends to cover a large distance, building up a momentum that can enable a lift higher than could normally be achieved with a greater angle of approach. The extreme wide-angle approach, however, decreases the economy of rotation over the bar, as the jumper wants to prolong their center of gravity at a high point.

This, of course, is contrary to efficient bar clearance. In the straight-on approach, the jumper is forced to stay erect before actually reaching the bar, and the mobility of the free leg is restricted through the lack of space needed to contribute levers of force in the upward drive.

Since the two extreme approach angles create difficulties, one would be wise to compromise—adopt an approach angle of approximately 25 to 35 degrees.

The speed of the run-up raises another issue. The Russians were perhaps the first to achieve success with extreme speeds. Thanks to their revolutionary weight-training programs, they also tended to have more leg strength than their counterparts.

Athletes must realize that velocity becomes more important as the bar goes higher, and that as the angle of approach is increased, more speed is needed to decrease the time spent over the bar. Strength is a prerequisite for those using a fast approach. This, along with hip positioning, must be developed for the athlete to capitalize on speed. When the athlete has difficulty exploiting speed due to lack of strength and coordination, a fast run-up becomes a detriment rather than an aid.

Knee flexion seems to be the key to transforming horizontal speed into vertical lift. When the take-off foot hits the track, the knee automatically bends with the weight of the jumper. Theoretically, the faster the approach, the greater the flexion of the knee. This action absorbs much of the run-up's forward momentum. A properly conditioned athlete is able to absorb and store this force in the manner of a steel spring. If the athlete lacks adequate strength, he'll naturally tend to kill his forward speed.

Any conscious effort to counteract the bending of the knee will yield unsatisfactory results. Little lift-off can be derived from jumping over a straight knee. Only a vaulting effect can be achieved, and this produces poor jumps as well as knee injuries. The proper jumping action requires a contraction of the thigh muscles produced only through knee flexion.

To assure a quick and efficient lifting action, the take-off foot must be correctly applied to the ground. The heel normally touches down first. The weight then shifts to the sole, then is immediately taken over by the ankle, knee, and hips (see John Dobroth photo 6-14). The transition must be effected smoothly and naturally. When the weight remains on the heel for any length of time, a braking action occurs.

Though a good deal of emphasis is placed on the coordination of the lead-leg spring with the upward force of the arms and shoulders, usually too little emphasis is placed upon the actual drive off the power foot. All too often, the jumper's efforts are limited due to the small amount of force derived from the plantar flexion of the take-off foot. There's simply too little accomplished by the jumping foot.

The forward ground speed also is related to the forward speed in the air. The long jumper provides the classic example of this principle: this athlete desires as much controlled speed as possible to carry forward momentum over into the horizontal flight.

With the high jumper, it becomes a matter of converting forward motion into vertical displacement, thus reducing the forward travel as much as possible but without eliminating it. The jumper's optimum approach speed should be great enough to put him or her across the bar at the peak of the lift rather than in front of or beyond the bar. This can be determined easily by a film study of the jumper.

The Take-Off

Russian research shows that the bending of the take-off leg on the last step decreases as the bar goes up. Dyatchkov reports that a jumper's leg at 6-7⅛ was flexed to 90 degrees prior to the take-off, and was decreased to 86 degrees at a jump of 6-10¾. The flexion of other jumpers' legs decreased from 98 to 88 degrees at similar changes in the bar.

This may mean that higher endeavors, the focus of energy conversion automatically becomes one of a speed impulse rather than time impulse. It may also mean a quicker swing up of the lead leg, which would naturally allow less time for the knee flexion and weight bearing on the take-off leg. The fact that the weight doesn't bear completely upon the take-off leg can actually increase the efficiency of the jump. The amount of weight is indicated by the angle of flexion in the trailing and power leg.

To exploit the speed of the run-up, it's therefore advantageous to begin the take-off with a forced upward hip motion *on the step before* the actual lift-off.

Dyatchkov indicates that the power (trailing) foot must be planted so that the heel touches the ground first, then the foot must immediately flatten out to assume the weight on the entire sole. The Russian also indicates the importance of moving the pelvis forward during the heel-foot transfer. This helps counteract the loss of valuable horizontal speed and converts speed into vertical lift.

After the foot assumes the correct position, the pelvis region must be positioned in front of a perpendicular line from the shoulders. This assures a more efficient centering of weight, as opposed to merely dropping the shoulders back at heel contact. In addition to being forward, the pelvis must be tilted slightly upward.

Another point of inerest lies in the relationship of the thighs during the swing step of the jump. Instead of the thighs being out of alignment during the last step, the athlete should keep them in close proximity to each other. At the moment the heel of the power foot contacts the ground, both thighs should be nearly parallel. This eliminates a dead spot when transferring speed into lift. (Fig. 6-1, 6-2).

FIGURE 6-1

First figure shows the jumper with thighs parallel, which tends to lessen the weight-bearing phase of the last step and helps roll the pelvis forward and upward. This shift in weight perpetuates speed from the run-up. The second figure shows the inefficient position and uneven weight distribution caused by split thighs.

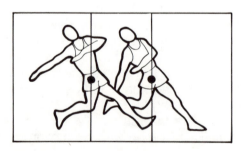

FIGURE 6-2

Clearly indicates correct position of hips in relation to shoulders. During last two steps, jumper must try to get hips in front of shoulders, and just prior to spring, he should let shoulders passively drop back even more. Though not expressed here, jumper, besides placing hips forward, moves pelvis actively upward. This seems to be one of the keys in perpetuating speed.

The Lead Leg

The efficiency of any jump stems from the action of the lead leg. It must be brought up quickly and forcefully. A deceleration at any point will transfer the pre-established momentum down to the lower body, virtually destroying the jumper's speed. (Fig. 6-3).

In a jump that doesn't have the benefit of a push-up from the power (jumping) foot, lift is developed by a hard, fast lead-leg kick. As the speed of the lead leg increases, there's displacement of the pelvis on that side of the body. This displacement tends to hold the body weight in line with the direct force of the take-off point.

If, however, the leg begins to slow on the upswing, there is no displacement and the muscle tension between the leading and the trail leg is lost. (Stretch adds to the contracting ability of a muscle.)

Straight-Leg vs. Bent-Leg Take-Off

Certain benefits can be derived from either the straight-leg or bent-leg take-off. The bent leg furnishes more speed plus the ability to transfer horizontal to vertical direction instantly. The straight leg allows more time for the leg to develop and maintain upward force.

The big problem of the straight leg lies in its inability to adequately exploit speed unless the pelvis, thighs and supple action of the power foot are utilized in conjunction with it.

The jumper may desire to combine the benefits of both styles. That is, use a bent leg in the early stages of the swing-up, then move quickly to a straight leg for added upward lift, then perhaps return to the bent leg upon nearing the high point of the jump. This tends to speed up rotation and furnish impetus to the movement down and away from the bar.

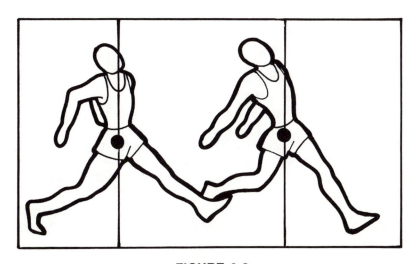

FIGURE 6-3

The Flop Style of High Jumping

The question "What style of high jump is more efficient?" is asked frequently. We are quite sure this question will be discussed for many years. However, one fact is quite evident. Nearly every new young jumper we see today is performing the flop as an accepted method of jumping. Most of these youngsters do not realize the mechanics and principles of why they use the flop, but there are underlying reasons for its acceptance.

First, the flop is much easier to learn and perhaps more fun. Speaking technically, a youth can achieve excellent results from this style of jump because it permits compensation for mistakes—the straddle style does not. In addition, the flop clearance is much less critical and easier to obtain than the conventional straddle rotation. Researchers tell us that the efficient circular take-off of the flop gives much greater height than the straight run-up. There is an inch to an inch-and-a-half more lift with the same leg strength and the same speed approach in a straight run-up. We have observed several outstanding jumpers who have cleared 2-4 inches more with a flop than with the straddle.

The flop, however, does not necessarily give the jumper a complete advantage. Again, researchers infer that the jumper's center of gravity in the straddle jump is slightly closer to the bar during clearance than in the back lay out of the flopper. This, of course, is an important factor in high jumping.

The flop, as we see it used by various athletes, is a combination of as many styles as you can conceive. In attempting to separate style into acceptable mechanics, it is necessary to isolate two major types of flop style.

The first is what could be called the power flop. The power flop is an off-shoot of the straddle jump style. It is characterized by a straight line approach with a noticeable lowering of the center of gravity on the last step prior to take off. For most athletes this style is unacceptable due to the great amount of strength necessary to get off the ground effectively. Mechanically, it is also impractical because one cannot take advantage of centrifugal force to aid in the conversion of horizontal velocity to vertical lift.

The effective jump style, the one I believe should be taught at all levels, is what is commonly called the speed flop. This specific type of jump currently is misunderstood somewhat. Therefore, we should identify the major mechanical skills of the approved take off and clearance.

Curved Run: In early descriptions of the approach, almost all writers professed the effectiveness of a half curve or double half curve approach (see Fig. 6-4):

FIGURE 6-4
Two Early Styles of Approach for the Flop

A.   The Double Circle-Two different arcs are plotted.
B.   The Single Circle-One single arc. Jumper leaves the ground near center of cross bar.

Generally, both of these approaches are considered ineffective because of inadequate approach speed. Also there is considerable difficulty in obtaining an identical and consistent pattern from jump to jump or competition to competition.

The single circle or an adaptation of the single circle is used for the power flop.

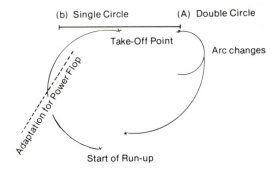

The semicircle curved run definitely will give the jumper more control during approach, but it also limits the horizontal speed. The primary disadvantage is that circular running creates considerable difficulty for the athlete in developing a definite stride pattern. This occurs not only in laying out the run-up but also in the actual practice of running the approach.

The "J" approach currently is considered the best and most effective way for a jumper to approach the bar. Three important reasons for this are:
- because of the initial straight line, the athlete can develop much more speed;
- the run-up is easily measured and laid out, consequently the consistency of steps is easily developed;
- it is a means of blending speed and centrifugal force. (Fig. 6-5)

Perhaps the number one consideration of the flop jump is that it utilizes centrifugal force. Without it, there can be no torque between foot and hips and hips and shoulder. Without these, take off is ineffective, as the athlete must revert solely to speed and strength.

It has been said many times that the run-up constitutes 80% of the total jump. If this is the case, and I believe it is, then at least 80% of training time should be spent on the runway and the run-up. Most problems occurring in the air and rotation are determined on the ground.

Concerns of the Approach for the Flop

There are three areas of concern in the approach to the flop:
- Speed of approach
- Centrifugal force
- Impulse at the instant of take off

To develop speed the athlete must always think gradual acceleration from start to jump. The coach or athlete listening to run-up cadence should be able to hear distinctly the pattern of the feet hitting the ground. The last three steps, however, should be so quick they are hardly discernable.

Obviously, the easiest way to achieve speed is to run in a straight line. The straight line of the flop approach is the stem of the J in our accepted style of run-up.

For the left-footed jumper, the run up is in a straight line at the pre-determined distance (radius) out from the standard. (see Fig. 6-5).

This predetermined distance is developed through experimentation. speed of the athlete generally is the determining factor setting the radius. The more speed, the wider the radius. The slower the athlete, the

FIGURE 6-5

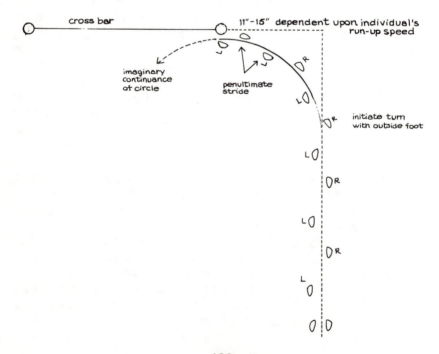

the 'j' approach utilized
for the speed flop

shorter the radius. It is important for the young, inexperienced to remember that running the curve is difficult; most novice jumpers tend to run two straight lines rather than a gentle curve. So, many times it is best to start with a wide radius because it is easy to negotiate while maintaining control and run-up velocity.

The run should be initiated so the athlete is taking from 9-11 total strides through the entire approach. The key, however, is to run so five steps are taken on the curve. Some coaches advocate four steps, but I prefer to initiate the turn with the outside foot as this lends itself to a curve rather than straight line running. The inside foot lead takes away a circular pivot point which initially established an angular momentum.

Summarized, the run should be a gradual and smooth build-up and ended fast, perhaps a little faster than the athlete feels he or she can use. The length of the run should insure near optimum velocity—too short a run will not allow speed and too long a run usually causes deceleration as well. The last five steps should be directed into a turn with the inside shoulder dropping into the middle of the circle.

The importance of centrifugal force must be understood by the athlete. this force (or angular momentum) specifically provides an advantage the flopper has over the straddle jumper. The effectiveness of angular momentum is really two-fold. First, when running a corner (curve) through the last five steps, the body from ankle to the shoulder is pulled into a torqued (twisted) position. The amount is dependent upon the angle of foot placement in relation to the bar. If the foot is placed parallel to the bar and the momentum of the upper body is still circular, there is a great deal of rotational force. Muscles from the ankle through the shoulder are placed on a stretch and there is a consequent *summation* of muscular force at the instant of take-off.

Secondly, angular momentum pulls the body inward away from the bar (Dwight Stones, photo 6-58). This action, coupled with the linear velocity of the run-up, forces the jump through the vertical axis and reduces eccentric thrust. Jumping through the vertical axis is perhaps the most sought after objective of any jumper. Without centrifugal force, the jumper's linear velocity would carry the athlete deep into the pit and is mechanically characterized as being a maximum amount of eccentric action, thus pulling the jumper out of the vertical alignment.

The third concern of the flopper is to develop an effective push against the ground at the instant of take-off. Impulse or ground reaction is the force developed equal and opposite to the force exerted by the jumper. Eker indicates it would be possible for a 160 pound jumper to increase his weight against the ground to over 600 pounds at the take-off. This great force from the ground up through the jumper's center of mass results from two major factors. Impulse actions are developed both with the leading knee and the arms. The knee is the most important. For an effective effort, the jumper's knee must be brought up quickly and flexed to provide speed. If the jumper can allow this leg to reach 90° or more and immediately stop the upward action (blocking it), a great deal more force is exerted against the ground.

The arms, a secondary but important impulse provider, are timed exactly with the knee, brought up flexed at the elbows through the vertical axis and immediately stopped at the chin, providing additional and simultaneous force (Dwight Stones, photos 6-62, 6-63).

Many times a jumper's arms will extend well up over the head upon take-off. The reasoning behind the arms' extension jump is that the center of mass is raised and thus it takes less effort to get off the ground. This is true, but there is a trade-off of effort versus force. It has been found that force provided by stopping knee and arms is more an advantage to the jumper than a high center of gravity.

At this point it is essential that the reader understand how impulse is employed during most track and field events.

It has been stated that increased force over a longer period of time is the key to providing impulse. It has recently been demonstrated that it is best to decrease the amount of time but increase the force. This applies to track and field events where a run-up is employed or when any of the predescribed "blocking" actions can be brought into play.

The speed flop run-up must culminate with a long-short pattern of the last two strides. The center of mass on the long stride is slightly dropped—the long step is called the penultimate stride and it is the key to effective center-of-mass placement in the jump. As the penultimate stride ceases the athlete moves into the final short approach step, the center of mass moves well up and the effect is actually a lessening of body weight due to the force of momentum. The object is to have 0 pounds of force acting in the downward position prior to any blocking. The less time spent on the ground the more effective the take off because it enables the athlete to maintain all or nearly all the linear velocity established during the run-up.

As described, the stride pattern is a long-short sequence. It is important that the athlete do everything in his means to establish this sequence. However, what generally is performed in anticipation to the take off is a gathering of the arms in hopes of developing force. That is, the arms are drawn back behind the body to generate a long upward thrust. this action simply destroys the ability to get off the ground quickly. Naturally, as the arms move back, so does the center of mass. This causes the jumping foot to strike the ground well ahead of the center of mass. Any time the foot strikes in advance of the body weight, linear velocity will decelerate.

The arms, and especially the outside arm, should not be allowed to move behind the body after the penultimate step. During the penultimate, when the inside leg is traveling forward, the outside arm is "posted" or held at the hip (Dwight Stones, photo 6-58). This not only keeps the center of mass forward, but it also causes a certain amount of upper body outward rotation, providing body torque between shoulders and hips. This stored muscle energy can be transferred to take-off force.

An additional key to a fast take off is the position and action of the leading leg moving into its upward thrust. As stated, it must be flexed but it also must be brought through under the body with the heel near the buttocks (Dwight Stones, photo 6-61). Many floppers drag the toe as the leading leg comes through. This fault is caused either by a too long last stride with the hips too low, or a stride frequency that has not accelerated over the last three steps.

WEEKLY WORKOUT FOR JUMPERS

NAME: DATE: 11/12/82

1. **Easy jogging**

2. **Warm-up drills:** a. High leg to 50 yds.;   b. Fast legs to 50 yds.;   c. 7x70 yds. aclerations; d. A-B-C's to 50 yds.;   e. Stretching

3. **Sprint belts**

4. **Stadium stairs**
   a. Sprinting up;   b. Sprinting down;
   c. Hopping up (1) Single leg, (2) Double leg;
   d. Hopping down (1) Single leg, (2) Double leg
   e. Hopping up ramp with vest

5. **Hill work**
   a. Protest (1) up, (2) down
   b. Ann Morrison (1) up, (2) down
   c. Americana (1) up, (2) down

6. **Flat drills**
   a Bounding R-L-R-L for height 7 step approach
   b. R leg hops with 7 step approach
   c. L leg hops with 7 step approach
   d. Giant bounding (90 out rather than up)
   e. R-R-L-L-R-R-L-L etc.
   f. Hop step jump step jump etc.

7. **Running drills**
   a. Seven step approach 5 hop test (1) R leg, (2) L leg
   b. Seven step approach hop-step-step-step-jump
   c. 3 step (1) Long Jump, (2) High Jump, (3) Triple Jump
   d. 5 step (1) Long Jump, (2) High Jump (3) Triple Jump
   e. Full run up (1) Long Jump, (2) High Jump, (3) Triple Jump
   f. Pop-ups (1) 3 step, (2) seven step
   g. HHH
   h. Side hill running

12. **Drop downs** a. 40, b. 50, c. 60, d. 70, e. 80, f. 100, g. 110, h. 165, i. 180, j. 220, k. 330, l. 352 m. 440, n. 500, o. 550, p. 600, q. 880, r. 1000

13. **Gun starts** (same letters as above)

14. **Continuous relays** (same letters as above)

15. a. Meet with coach
    b. Films study
    c. Picture

16. **Workout of your choice**

17. **Warm-up and check marks only**

18. **Pool** a. swimming, b. intervals of shallow, c. intervals of deep

M   Same as Sprinters

Tu (1 To 320)(2a Slow & Fast To 40 x 4 ea)
(3 Step Take Off Drill x 10 To 40)
(7a(1) & (2) x 6 ea Leg)(+ea x 4 for Time)
(4E x 6 Full Distance R-R-L-L-L-L x 6)
(4C Low Deck & 6 ea Leg)(100 yds. Hop ea Leg x 1)

W   Same as Sprinters

Th   Same as Sprinters

8. Boxes
  a. 14-16' bounding R-L-R-L; 16-18 bounding R-L-R-L
  b. RR-LL
  c. Single leg through both legs
  d. HJ drills (1) Table jumping, (2) Ground to box to ground jumping, (3) Ground to low box jump
  e. Long jump drills (1) ground to box to ground jump, (2) ground to low box jump

9. Weights
  a. Special (1) clean & jerk, (2) single leg squats, (3) weighted vest, (4) lead leg drill
  b. Circuit
  c. Power strength (general)

10. Running sets a. 40, b. 50, c. 60, d. 70, e. 80, f. 100, g. 110, h. 165, i. 180, j. 220, k. 330, l. 352, m. 440, n. 500, o. 550, p. 600, q. 880, r. 1000

11. Hurdles (same letters as above)

F Full Warm-up (Include Everything)
1 × 352 Trial
To Weight Room - Full Lifting

S Jog 3-4 Miles

S

Weight Comments: Jump Day (Mon or Tues)
(1 To 320) (2 Slow + Fast × 4) (3 Step Take-off
Drills) (Jumping - Start 4 steps × 2
                            5 steps × 2
                            6 steps × 2
Emphase i.e. King 7 steps × 2
Problems Line of Steps 9 steps × 2
Jake-Knee - AoB - Run-up
    4× Box Jump + Short Approach

6-7   6-6   6-5

6-13   6-12   6-11

DWIGHT STONES, U.S.A.

6-4   6-3   6-2   6-1

6-10   6-9   6-8

6-19   6-18   6-17

6-25   6-24

6-30   6-29   6-28

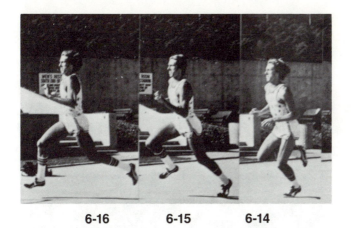

6-16   **6-15**   **6-14**

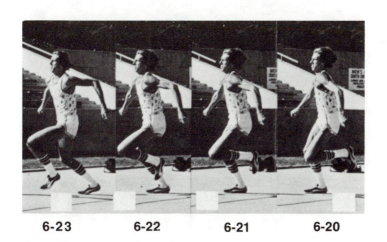

6-23   **6-22**   **6-21**   **6-20**

6-27   **6-26**

6-37   **6-36**   **6-35**

6-41   **6-40**

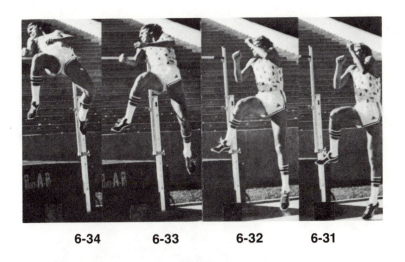

6-34   6-33   6-32   6-31

6-39   6-38

JOHN DEBROTH, U.S.A.

6-1   6-2   6-3

6-6   6-7

6-11   6-12   6-13

6-4   6-5

6-8   6-9   6-10

6-14   6-15

6-16 6-17 6-18

6-21 6-22 6-23

6-27 6-28 6-29

6-19   6-20

6-24   6-25   6-26

6-30   6-31   6-32

7

Long Jump

The long jump is perhaps the most neglected event in track and field, perhaps because it appears so simple. However, the coach should realize that an effective jump takes only .12 of a second to clear the take-off board. In this short period the athlete must make adjustments in the center of gravity, velocity, foot placement, and the upper and lower leg; it becomes a very compelx event.

In building from the simple to the complex, the most important factor in the long jump is horizontal velocity which contributes more distance to the jump than vertical velocity by a 2-1 ratio. Therefore, everything possible should be done in the run-up and plant to conserve horizontal speed.

The Runway

The natural goal for the long jumper is to run at near top speed and be able to hit the board with no disruption of that run-up velocity.

It should be remembered that most problems of stride consistency occur in the first 3-4 strides of the run-up. In order for stride consistency to become second nature to the athlete, a necessity, it must be worked on frequently.

Another general factor borne out by experience is simply that stride patterns *do* change somewhat throughout the season. One reason to train each day is to develop speed and strength. As these two components change, so will stride patterns. I have had good success telling jumpers to begin the early season using a short approach. True, there will be less speed in the run-up, but there is far less chance of stride error when reaching the board. As stride becomes more consistent, the jumper should gradually increase the run-up length.

As has been stated in numerous other places in this book, it takes a minimum of 5 seconds (and for the superior athlete 6 seconds) to reach maximum speed. It is also known that world-class long jumpers use approximately 95% of their maximum speed during the actual long jump run-up. Calculating 5 or 6 seconds, maximum speed would be reached at 150-180 feet. However, in the horizontal jumps, we are more concerned with usable speed. This decreases the runway to around 150-160 feet. Most jumpers utilize from 110-130 feet. They may well be advised to increase run-up distances.

In coaching jumpers over the years, I have attempted to get away from specific distances on the runway. Rather, the runway length is determined by a set number of strides from start to the board. The approach should be from 17-24 strides. Early in the season the athlete uses 17 strides and later will use 22-24. Thus, the distance may change due to strength and speed, but the stride rhythm will not.

Establishing a Stride Pattern

To determine the length of run, always use the take-off foot for all checking references. In addition, do all preliminary work from the board back into the runway. If the athlete is a left-footed jumper, tell him to stand at the board with the right foot in contact. From a standing start, the athlete builds into a full speed spring while the coach counts the steps. When using a 17 step approach, count 9 strides and mark (should be the left foot). This is your last check mark. Eight additional steps will be needed to reach the board. The athlete continues for these 8 steps and takes a hop off the left foot to emulate the take-off. There should be two check marks: one at the start and one 9 strides from the start.

Now measure the distance from the start to the hop and also the intermediate check mark. Place the athlete at the opposite end of the runway and have him perform the exact stride sequence as he did from the board. An observer should be assigned at the board and at the intermediate check point. The jumper should make the steps at these points several times to identify a range of tendencies. After several run-throughs, you have an excellent guide to an established runway.

Two cautionary notes should be observed. First, the athlete should not attempt to hit marks, but instead run naturally so a pattern will develop. Second, at each 17th step (at the point where the toe board should be) the athlete must hop into the air. This will bring into account the penultimate and drive step which will follow a different pattern than the normal run. Warn the athlete not to change stride pattern to hit the board. All changes should be reflected by adjustment in the check marks. The development of the 22-24 step run-up would be developed in the same manner.

The ninth stride check mark (regardless of the numbers of steps in the approach) is extremely important because this indicates the athlete is on target. If he or she is, there should be no regard to anything including hitting the board, other than maintaining horizontal speed. If by chance the athlete misses the 9th check mark, there will be time to stop completely before fouling.

The emphasis during the last 8 steps should be on fast arms, high knee lift and a high level focal point of the head and eyes.

A long jumper should never hear the word settle. The hips should not noticeably drop in preparing for the jump. Two steps out the jumper should stretch slightly into the penultimate stride. This lengthening varies only from 3-6 inches. During this time a slight lowering of the hips will occur, but it will not detract from horizontal speed. The jumping stride, on the other hand, will be slightly shorter (again 3-6"). This tends to speed the athlete up over the board and raises the center of gravity. The shorter the time on the board, the better. The last four steps should be: even distance -even distance - slightly longer - slightly shorter. This is the key to an effective run-up. (Fig. 7-1)

Take-Off Principles

Without question, the most important factor at take-off is impulse. We learned many years ago that all track and field events are the application of force over a period of time. Impulse, of course, is defined as force x time. Throughout the years, it has been felt that the more time-force which can be applied the better. Recently, however, work with forceplates has shown that with less time, more force can be created.

It has been wrongly assumed that a jumper should attempt to maximize both the magnitude of vertical force and the time which this force acts against the ground. This is not true. Research demonstrates that the time of take-off, and time during which vertical forces can be applied, will decrease as the distance or height of the jump increases.

In the long jump take-off, this is exactly what we try to accomplish, a very quick application of force. The champion long jumper's foot contact with the board is .12 of a second. The novice or ineffective jumper's foot contact may be as much as .18-.20 of a second.

How to Decrease Time application and Increase Downward Force

1. High center of gravity just before and at instant of jump
   A. Run, jump or hop with speed and upright body
   B. Run on toes
   C. Pelvis (hips) tucked and pressed forward
2. Lead leg must be quick (flexed fully at knee). The heel will come close to buttocks after clearing the ground.

FIGURE 7-1
17 Stride Pattern Approach Plan
for Establishing Steps

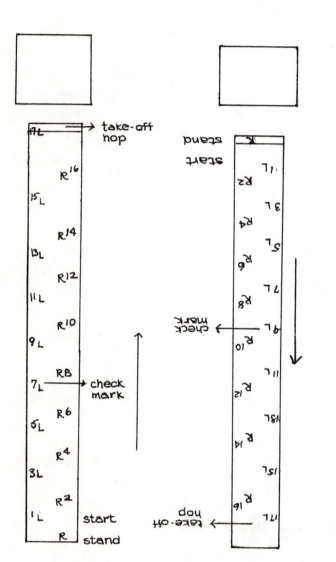

step 1
running back
from pit to determine
running distance

step 2
running from
actual take-off
point toward pit

3. Jab (punch-like) action of the arms. Drive hard to chin then *block or stop* upward motion. This provides greater impulse on the ground.
4. Free arms and legs must move at maximum velocity while the athlete is in contact with ground. Any acceleration after the instant of take-off cannot add to vertical velocity.

In addition, but along the same lines, impulse contributes to and is aided by horizontal displacement. According to Dyson, horizontal displacement is more important than vertical displacement. An athlete running a 100 yard dash in 11.0 seconds would jump 23'6" by raising their center of gravity 2'6". On the other hand, an athlete who is running 10.5 for the 100 yards would jump 25'5" by raising the center of gravity 2'6". As was stated in the first paragraph, horizontal velocity is 2 to 1 in importance in gaining distance in the long jump.

At the board all body segments must generate forward and upward force simultaneously. Any moving body segment produces force in an opposite direction (Newton's 3rd Law). For example, any upward arm movement produces a downward force against the runway. Conversely, any backward arm movement (at the hip) will produce a forward force. Therefore, body segments moving in any direction when controlled and blocked (stopped) at a certain point will produce a good amount of transference of momentum (impulse).

Also worthy of note is that deceleration of any body segment while in motion produces a force in the same direction as the original acceleration. The classic example here is a passenger riding in a car that suddenly stops, i.e. decelerates. The passenger is thrown forward. When a long jumper plants the foot to jump, there is a certain amount of deceleration and a subsequent forward rotation of the upper body. In mechanics this is called the hinge principle. Forward rotation to the horizontal jumper is a negative effect, obviously one to be minimized. In other events, however, an athlete utilizes the hinge effect for superior performance.

The final consideration for foot contact is that the higher the vertical movement of the center of mass (hips), the less time for foot contact. A statement to this effect was already made in relation to impulse time off the board. However, the center of mass height will determine the parabolic curve off the board. A low center of mass yields a curve like Fig. 7-2A; a high center of mass produces a curve illustrated by Fig. 7-2B. The latter naturally leads to maintenance of horizontal velocity.

FIGURE 7-2

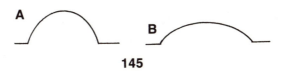

Skill "Keys" for the Effective Long Jump

Foot Plant:

The athlete should land on the full, flat foot, not the ball only and not the toe only. However, the toe should touch the ground first. With the full-foot landing, you create an additional, "quick" eccentric contraction of the achilles tendon. Too often the stretch occurs over a too long period of time. The quicker the stretch, the more powerful the contraction. Don't forget that the achilles and the gastroc areas are the key jump muscles.

The Compression Phase:

During this phase of the take-off, the period of maximum eccentric muscular contraction takes place. Again, the quicker this occurs the more powerful the stretch reflexes. Quickness here is probably dependent upon the active (pawing) foot action during the contact with the board. Many times athletes simply allow their forward momentum to carry them through the compression phase. This tendency, however, takes too long and many phases of the take-off are disrupted.

The position of the free leg has much to do with the time of support of the take-off foot. The free leg should never be trailing the hips too far and, more importantly, the heel should come through high in relation to the buttocks (Fig. 7-3)

FIGURE 7-3

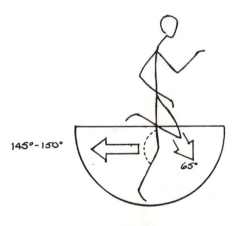

145°- 150°

65°

The support leg should have flexion angle of 145-150° and the free leg at 65°. This approximate angle will provide the contractile force and quickness necessary for an active lift from the board. Regarding the angle of the support leg, anything less than 145-150° will supply the knee with too much force and it will continue bending or buckle, thus destroying forward momentum. On the other hand, too much flexion means that the leg cannot extend quickly enough to give complete power before the foot clears the toe board.

For additional force off the board, the athlete should toe-in slightly allowing the leg to assume a fuller extended position. This is due to nature's alignment of the femur and the tibia.

Upper Body Position at Take-Off:
The line of force acts through the support foot, through the hips and center of mass. It is not through the upper body. Thus, the upper body must be vertical and not forward as many believe. Any forward lean seems only to increase unwanted forward rotation. To assure this vertical alignment, the most prominent factor is the focal point and position of the head. Throughout the jump, the eyes and head should remain parallel to the ground except just prior to landing.

Arm Action at Take-Off:
The opposite arm to the free leg must accelerate with a 90° bend of the elbow (this allows the fastest possible angle). The key is to stop the hand immediately at the head. If possible it is stopped (blocked) and quickly dropped, providing maximum transference of momentum. The arm on the same side of the take-off leg should also be flexed at 90° accelerated, then quickly stopped at the hip. This is in conjunction with the other arm and provides an equal amount of usable force. (Fig. 7-4) (Igor Ter Ovanesyan 19-20 does not block with back arm)

All these actions maintain a fast, powerful movement off the board. This, without question, is the major part of the long jump. Most of the athlete's training should be directed toward the run-up and the actions that are to take place on the board.

FIGURE 7-4

147

Technique in the Air:

Basically there are two principle concerns for the jumper while in mid-air. First, some means of movement should be employed to help prevent unwanted forward rotation. Second, some action must be taken to provide an efficient landing; that is, to gain as much distance as absolutely possible.

To date, with the exception of the somersault (which is probably the most effective but illegal), there are three styles most athletes use: the sail, the hang, and the hitchkick.

The sail is unacceptable because it increases forward rotation.

The hang style of jump is acceptable, especially for the beginning jumper who does not gain enough distance to complete the hitchkick. In this style the arms are brought to an overhead position with as much back arch as possible, thus delaying (somewhat) the inevitable forward rotation. But rotation is only delayed—not counteracted.

The hitchkick is the most efficient style. It is difficult for the beginner to learn but when mastered, the jumper gains tremendous benefits. Authorities on mechanics tell us that as a jump is taken from a horizontal movement an axis of rotation is a natural outcome. This rotation is called axis of momentum. If a secondary axis can be developed by an area of the body that has a moderate amount of mass, the original rotation can be absorbed; the more mass, the more absorption that can take place. Therefore, if while in the air, a secondary rotational axis with the arms is established a small amount of forward rotation can be absorbed. However, if the athlete utilizes both arms and legs, a large amount of body weight has been brought into play and a large amount of forward rotation is counteracted.

The hitchkick is described as an almost continual cycling or windmilling of the arms and legs while in flight. More simply, one-and-a-half to two steps in the air. While employing this continual arm-leg movement it is important to remember that the longer (more extended) the arms and legs, the more effective the technique. The length of the levers contribute to a strong secondary axis.

Landing:

I consider landing begins when the athlete is still in the air, just coming out of the chosen jump style. If the jumper is utilizing the hitchkick, at the instant the cycling action ceases the athlete benefits by raising and extending the legs as completely as possible. At that time the head should be forcefully brought down to the thighs. This serves as a two-way action, for as the head is brought down, the legs will rise and as the legs rise, the head comes down (Newton's Third Law of Motion).

The arms work in conjunction with the head; they swing from behind and over the top down to and past the legs. The added mass of the arms also serves to raise the legs. The arms do not stay in front of the body, however. By utilizing our knowledge of the center of gravity and the parabolic curve, we understand that if the arms are positioned behind the body, the center of mass moves back and since the center of gravity is following an unchangeable flight pattern (parabolic curve), the entire body shifts forward. In moving the arms behind the body, the jumper gains approximately 6-8" on the jump.

When the feet have contacted the pit, both arms must be brought forcefully to keep the athlete from falling backward.

The "trotter" landing is perhaps the best method of maintaining balance in the pit. In this method one leg continues to be extended while the other is relaxed. When contact is made, the stiff leg serves as a lever and spins the body in over the relaxed leg, allowing the hips to land on one side well ahead of the feet.

Better control, stability and balance are achieved in the landing when the feet are 12-18 inches apart. In addition, the hips can move through rather than over the knees as occurs when the feet are together. The latter technique would occur if the jumper is utilizing a "bounce or scoop" landing technique.

The key for perfecting the landing is to dissipate completely all forward momentum generated through run-up and jump. If the athlete is bounding out of the pit, then momentum is not being utilized—certainly a mistake.

WEEKLY WORKOUT FOR JUMPERS

NAME: Long Jump (All)   **DATE:** 4/16/82

1. **Easy jogging**

2. **Warm-up drills:** a. High leg to 50 yds.;   b. Fast legs to 50 yds.;   c. 7x70 yds. accelerations; d. A-B-C's to 50 yds.;   e. Stretching

3. **Sprint belts**

4. **Stadium stairs**
   a. Sprinting up;   b. Sprinting down;
   c. Hopping up (1) Single leg, (2) Double leg;
   d. Hopping down (1) Single leg, (2) Double leg

5. **Hill work**
   a. Protest (1) up, (2) down
   b. Ann Morrison (1) up, (2) down
   c. Americana (1) up, (2) down

6. **Flat drills**
   a Bounding R-L-R-L for height 7 step approach
   b. R leg hops with 7 step approach
   c. L leg hops with 7 step approach
   d. Giant bounding (90 out rather than up)
   e. R-R-L-L-R-R-L-L etc.
   f. Hop step jump step jump etc.
   g. Single leg for 100 yds.

12. **Drop downs** a. 40, b. 50, c. 60, d. 70, e. 80, f. 100, g. 110, h. 165, i. 180, j. 220, k. 330, l. 352 m. 440, n. 500, o. 550, p. 600, q. 880, r. 1000

13. **Gun starts** (same letters as above)

14. **Continuous relays** (same letters as above)

15. a. Meet with coach
    b. Films study
    c. Picture

16. **Workout of your choice**

17. **Warm-up and check marks only**

18. **Pool** a. swimming, b. intervals of shallow, c. intervals of deep

M (1 to 1320) (Stretching - 15 min) (2a-b-c x 4 ea. to 80) (7I x 12, 7J x 12) (8E with 7 step x 8) (10J x 6) (9 full)

Tu (1 to 1320) (Stretch -15 min) (12E x 6) (4a x 5 for time) (4C (1) x 8 ea. leg) (6G x 3 ea. leg) (cool down)

7. Running drills

   a. Seven step approach 5 hop test (1) R leg,
      (2) L leg

   b. Seven step approach hop-step-step-step-jump

   c. 3 step (1) Long Jump, (2) High Jump, (3) Triple
      Jump

   d. 5 step (1) Long Jump, (2) High Jump (3) Triple
      Jump

   e. Full run up (1) Long Jump, (2) High Jump,
      (3) Triple Jump

   f. Pop-ups (1) 3 step, (2) seven step

   g. HHH

   h. Side hill running

   i. 12 step runway

   j. 14 step runway

8. Boxes

   a. 14-16' bounding R-L-R-L; 16-18 bounding
      R-L-R-L

   b. RR-LL

   c. Single leg through both legs

   d. HJ drills (1) Table jumping, (2) Ground to box to
      ground jumping, (3) Ground to low box jump

   e. Long jump drills (1) ground to box to ground
      jump, (2) ground to low box jump

9. Weights

   a. Special (1) clean & jerk, (2) single leg squats,
      (3) weighted vest, (4) lead leg drill

   b. Circuit

   c. Power strength (general)

10. Running sets a. 40, b. 50, c. 60, d. 70, e. 80,
   f. 100, g. 110, h. 165, i. 180, j. 220, k. 330,
   l. 352, m. 440, n. 500, o. 550, p. 600, q. 880, r. 1000

11. Hurdles (same letters as above)

W (1 to 1320) (Stretch -15 min)
(2a-b-c × 4 ea to 80) (10K × 3 drop down
(9 full) (Easy Jogging)

Th (1 to 1320) (Stretch - 15 min)
(2a-b-c × 9 ea. to 60) (7 full approach
× 3-sets of 3 with Pop) (10H × 4)(10E × 4)

F Travel- full warm up
full run-up, Mark steps &
Run through with Pop.

S Compete -Trials 12:00
             Finals 1:00

S Easy Distance Run
or Swim

Weight
Comments:

IGOR TER-OVANESYAN, U.S.S.R. COPYRIGHT © 1970, PHIL BATH

    7-19   7-18   7-17   7-16   7-15

| 7-5 | 7-4 | 7-3 | 7-2 |

| 7-10 | 7-9 | 7-8 | 7-7 | 7-6 |

| 7-14 | 7-13 | 7-12 | 7-11 |

7-26   **7-25**   **7-24**

7-32   **7-31**   **7-30**

7-36   **7-35**

7-23　　　　**7-22**　　　　**7-21**　　　　**7-20**

7-29　　　　**7-28**　　　　**7-27**

7-34　　　　**7-33**

7-41   **7-40**   **7-39**

7-46   **7-45**

7-38   7-37

7-44   7-43   7-42

7-50   7-49

7-55   7-54   7-53

7-48   **7-47**

7-52   **7-51**

8

Triple Jump

To many, the triple jump is the most complex event in track and field. Perhaps this is true; however, by carefully analyzing each individual phase and the mechanics involved, it can be taught effectively and learned even by youngsters.

Experience has shown this event is more natural than any except running events. I have used the triple jump and triple jump drills including box jumping and plyometrics with elementary school boys and girls. The learning response was much more effective than any other field event with which I have worked. Hopping, skipping and even spaced jumps are natural playtime activities for most, if not all, young kids.

The Key: HORIZONTAL SPEED

Just as in the long jump, the distance attained in the triple jump is dependent upon horizontal velocity developed in the run-up approach. However, we have additional problems which begin at the take-off of the first phase (hop); for at this point velocity must be maintained, controlled and, most importantly, distributed over the additional two phases of the jump.

One must understand that foot placement in relation to the center of gravity is the key factor in controlling and maintaining speed throughout the three phases of the jump.

The more advanced the foot strike from the center of gravity, the greater the loss of speed. Therefore, it would be ideal to gain a slightly low take-off angle (of center for gravity) and a steep high landing for at least the first two phases of the event. The low angle take-off conserves horizontal speed as does the high angle landing. However, if the reader understands the principle of the parabolic curve, he knows that the angle developed off the ground will determine the angle coming back to the ground. Therefore, if the athlete leaves the hop with a low angle he also will come back with a low angle; consequently, the landing foot will strike the ground well ahead of the center of mass.

The jumper must do something to compensate for the advanced foot placement and the low landing angle. This compensation is effectively accomplished with an *active* pawing or grabbing action of the lead foot at the instant of ground contact. In essence, the jumper pulls the body forward with the fast, powerful "pawing action." It is important to note that without this active foot action, the jumper will be jolted to a near stop through each phase of the jump. The active foot must be initiated just before and continue through the weight bearing support phase of that leading leg. This action, although many times neglected, is the key for maintaining speed.

Specified Skill Characteristics

It is very difficult to train an athlete in a distinct method of triple jumping as there will always be individual differences. However, in categorizing specific styles, I have found it much easier to give directions and suggest changes which would cause consistency in jumping patterns.

The basic difference in triple jumping styles is how the athlete utilizes speed and how much deceleration occurs over the three phases of the total jump.

Although one can divide triple jumping styles into three or four types, it should be remembered there are really only two true choices for the athlete to accept. The first emphasizes upward velocity and thus lessens momentum. The second accepts a lower flight pattern, and thus maintains momentum but loses some height.

When analyzing the two choices, one must consider individual characteristics of the jumper in determining style. The primary factor is the innate leg speed of the athlete. If the athlete possesses a good amount of speed then the "flat" style momentum emphasis is more effective. If, on the other hand, the athlete has only average speed, he probably should point toward the high hop and step method jump style. It should be remembered, however, that this style is suited to an athlete who is willing to develop a great amount of strength and flexibility.

The Polish or Flat Style of Jumping

This style came into prominence through the jumping of Josef Schmidt, who was the world record holder from 1960-68 and who had a best of 55'10". Schmidt originally started his career as a high first-phase jumper. But by evaluating his individual characteristics, he found an ingredient most jumpers did not possess—speed. He had 10.5 100 meter sprint speed.

Wishing to utilize his sprinting ability, he gave priority to the development of momentum. He worked to stay low and reduce his normal first phase from 21' to about 19 and ½ feet. The primary tendencies of the flat style are:

- The jumper lands with the support foot more directly under the center of gravity (approximately a foot in front of the hips), thus maintaining horizontal speed.
- Next the athlete wishes to increase the distance of the second phase (step) while staying as low as possible. This is done with the *active foot* landing well ahead of the hips.
- Finally, the athlete makes an all-out effort to convert speed into vertical lift during the last phase.

Ideally the athlete employing this jump style would be around 35-30-35% ratio for all three phases. The advantage of the Polish style is speed conservation, but the disadvantage is difficulty in maintaining balance in flight and during the landing. Usually the Polish style jumper will utilize a single arm action throughout the entire series. *The single arm jumper will always have trouble remaining balanced and controlled.*

There are various disadvantages to the single arm style of jumping. Impulse, which is basic to any momentum transference, should occur simultaneously with the arms and legs. Many times the coordination is not possible as the hip and leg buckle when one arm is forward and the other back. This unbalanced position causes rotation and pulls the ultimate forces out of alignment. There is also a tendency for the foot to strike the ground prematurely as the body goes into unwanted forward rotation when one arm moves ahead of the center of mass.

The Soviet Double Arm Style

Basically, this method or style is characterized by a high hop and step with a tendency toward a flat jump phase. The method was developed by the Russians and best used by Viktor Saneyev (see total film sequence), who has exceeded 57 feet and captured three Olympic championships.

Currently this is the most copied jumping style in the world. More importantly, it is the most practical style as it provides maximum transference of momentum. It also suits all jump drills, even those utilized by non-triple jumpers. Therefore, this style of jump is the basis for a common training system for most track and field athletes.

The most important aspect of this style is utilization of both arms (double arm) throughout the entire sequence. Until the 1970's most jumpers used a single arm, at least on the hop, and many jumpers continued the single arm into the second and third phases, because it tended to maintain horizontal momentum. However, after experimentation it was found that certain advantages could be achieved with the double arm along with maintaining speed through the jump phases.

In earlier discussions concerning center of mass and foot placement we talked about not being able to change the parabola after the athlete leaves the ground. This is still true, but adjustments can be made to alter the center of gravity position. The athlete can shift the center of mass either forward or backward by changing arm and leg positions in flight. For example, by moving both arms back behind the body in an extended position, the center of mass will also move back (by as much as 6 inches). By adjusting the center of mass back, the athlete will prolong the time spent in the air and thus increase the hop-step and jump distances. It is therefore important to remember that getting both arms back and high will increase distance without disrupting momentum appreciably. (Fig. 8-21)

In addition to the above principle, there are additional benefits of using the double arm principle. Impulse or transference of force is at least doubled when arms are moving forward into the blocking position rather than a single arm. It is much easier to work the lead leg and both arms together than with one arm forward and the other back. One can correct most balance problems occurring during the single arm style.

FIGURE 8-1

162

With the double arm, lateral rotation is largely eliminated. Finally, perhaps the biggest problem in any horizontal jumping event is that of forward rotation when leaving the ground after a run-up. With both arms back, however, the jumper changes the axis of momentum and therefore reduces forward rotation.

It should be mentioned that certain problems do exist with the double arm style of jumping. Perhaps the biggest difficulty is adjusting the arms from the normal running style to the unnatural double arm style. Usually there is a definite reduction of speed while the athlete is learning the double arm. Consequently, you can expect a jumper's distance to decrease for a period of time when and if there is a transition in styles.

When a jumper doubles as a long jumper-triple jumper, a decision must be reached in regard to using the single arm or the double arm. The long jumper will definitely have more speed off the board using the straight single arm block. But the long jumper does not have to worry about keeping momentum through two additional phases of a jump that a triple jumper does. It is difficult for the doubling athlete to use one style for one jump and another for the other event.

Teaching the Double Arm

The big problem with the double arm take-off for the hop is that most athletes allow the opposite arm to drift behind the hips as is the natural tendency when running. The effective double arm is initiated one-and-one-half steps away from the board. If taught properly the athlete, instead of allowing the arm to go back behind the hip, bounces the hand off the stomach which allows it immediately to come up *in time with* the lead arm (see Saneyev, photos 8-8, 8-9, 8-10).

Runway Considerations

As horizontal velocity is the key to effective jumping, so a major portion of a jumper's effectiveness is attributed to what occurs on the runway prior to the jump.

Many questions are asked concerning the length of the runway. To answer these the coach and athlete should go back and review the principles of acceleration in the chapter on Sprinting.

A world class sprinter will not achieve full momentum until accelerating for nearly 6 seconds. A youngster or a runner of lesser ability will reach top speed sooner than 6 seconds. However, the range is still in the neighborhood of 5 seconds; 5-6 seconds equal a 135-180 foot run-up. Needless to say, this would be an extreme distance for a run-up approach, but most jumpers underestimate the importance of speed during the approach. Maybe it would prove beneficial for the athlete to use greater runway distances.

Research also shows that a world class long jumper will use approximately 95% sprint speed on the runway. Regardless of the athlete's speed (fast or slow) we seek that 95% range.

To determine the athlete's efficiency in using speed, they sprint over 60 yards and are timed the last 20 yards to a *hop* off the board (Fig. 8-2).

If the athlete is much slower than 2.62, some major corrections must be made in the last 7 steps or in the penultimate (settling) into the board. The last 6-7 steps or twenty yards is the real key to reaching optimum sprint through the jump.

As has been stated earlier, settling is a term that should be eliminated from coaching. What the jumper seeks is a slightly increased distance during the penultimate step and a slightly shorter step during the ultimate (last) step. This maintains horizontal velocity and raises the center of gravity for the take-off.

FIGURE 8-2

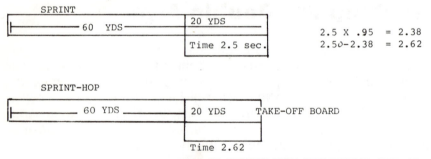

THIS IS OPTIMUM TIME UTILIZATION OVER 20 YDS

Total Jump Considerations

In a recent publication, *the Triple Jump Encyclopedia* by Ernie Bullard and Larry Knuth, the "perfect jump" is described. The authors summarized the success of the jump in three basic areas:
- The acceleration off the board.
- The focal eye contact (balance and body posture)
- The timing of the arm and leg movements

We have already discussed the total run-up approach; however, acceleration off the board is developed from 6-8 steps out away from the board. Characteristically, all long jumpers, pole vaulters and triple jumpers begin a gradual deceleration when their attention moves away from the run-up and into the take-off. Therefore, it is of utmost importance that from 35-45 feet away from the board everything is pointed toward acceleration with no letup in that attitude. The key to this last stage approach is increased arm action and emphasis on high knees with the focal point up parallel to the runway.

At the take-off, it is important to consider a low trajectory to maintain speed through all phases of the jump. The lead leg must be driven low and forward and the arms (double arm style) come through with the palms down (see Saneyev, photos 8-26, 8-27). This keeps the arm impulse out rather than up. If working the single arm, it is important to stop (block) the arm at the chin. This increases impulse and provides a quicker and more forceful movement off the board.

During the flight of the hop, the head and body must remain vertical with the focal point still parallel to the ground.

Because of the nature of the hop (take-off on one leg and landing on the same) a circular leg action takes place. During this leg action, it is important that both arms move back into an extended position as near to shoulder height as possible. This action has a dual purpose. First it delays forward rotation; and second, it moves the center of gravity back and allows the foot to pick up additional distance before contacting the ground.

The hop landing is primary to determining the success of the step and jump. The athlete seeks as much distance on the hop landing as will allow speed and force to carry him effectively into the step (no farther). To insure speed and force the foot must be dorsi flexed and immediately before landing must begin an active pawing motion. This coupled with a simultaneous forward movement of the high straight arms, which are again brought up blocked with the palms down, will sustain impulse and speed. The trajectory on the step phase still should be low to maintain velocity.

To insure this low trajectory, the lead knee is brought through low and forward with the foreleg ahead of and not behind the knee. The driving foreleg is then flexed under the knee with the thigh kept nearly parallel to the ground until landing. This single but important movement will allow greater distance on the step with no additional effort (see Saneyev, photos 8-30, 8-31, 8-32).

Moving from the step to the jump, the athlete seeks the same high backward arm movement as accomplished in the hop and step. It is at this time that we change from horizontal to vertical emphasis. The only real difference between the triple jump (jump phase) and the long jump is the time factor. For most triple jumpers there is insufficient time to complete the full-fledged hitch kick. Most jumpers go into a sail or a hang style jump. Naturally the hang (and if possible the hitch kick) are the most efficient styles of in-air technique because they displace forward rotation in the landing. During the landing and only during the landing is the head allowed to move out of the level plane. It should now be pushed down vigorously toward the knees. This, through the equal-opposite reaction principle, tends to move the legs up prior to landing.

WEEKLY WORKOUT FOR JUMPERS

NAME: Triple Jump (All)   **DATE:** 10/5/82

1. **Easy jogging**

2. **Warm-up drills:** a. High leg to 50 yds.;   b. Fast legs to 50 yds.;   c. 7x70 yds. acclerations; d. A-B-C's to 50 yds.;   e. Stretching

3. **Sprint belts**

4. **Stadium stairs**
   a. Sprinting up;   b. Sprinting down;
   c. Hopping up (1) Single leg, (2) Double leg;
   d. Hopping down (1) Single leg, (2) Double leg

5. **Hill work**
   a. Protest (1) up, (2) down
   b. Ann Morrison (1) up, (2) down
   c. Americana (1) up, (2) down

6. **Flat drills**
   a Bounding R-L-R-L for height 7 step approach
   b. R leg hops with 7 step approach
   c. L leg hops with 7 step approach
   d. Giant bounding (90 out rather than up)
   e. R-R-L-L-R-R-L-L etc.
   f. Hop step jump step jump etc.

7. **Running drills**
   a. Seven step approach 5 hop test (1) R leg, (2) L leg
   b. Seven step approach hop-step-step-step-jump
   c. 3 step (1) Long Jump, (2) High Jump, (3) Triple Jump
   d. 5 step (1) Long Jump, (2) High Jump (3) Triple Jump
   e. Full run up (1) Long Jump, (2) High Jump, (3) Triple Jump
   f. Pop-ups (1) 3 step, (2) seven step
   g. HHH
   h. Side hill running

8. **Boxes**
   a. 14-16' bounding R-L-R-L; 16-18 bounding R-L-R-L
   b. RR-LL
   c. Single leg through both legs
   d. HJ drills (1) Table jumping, (2) Ground to box to ground jumping, (3) Ground to low box jump
   e. Long jump drills (1) ground to box to ground jump, (2) ground to low box jump

12. **Drop downs** a. 40, b. 50, c. 60, d. 70, e. 80, f. 100, g. 110, h. 165, i. 180, j. 220, k. 330, l. 352 m. 440, n. 500, o. 550, p. 600, q. 880, r. 1000

13. **Gun starts** (same letters as above)

14. **Continuous relays** (same letters as above)

15. a. Meet with coach
    b. Films study
    c. Picture

16. **Workout of your choice**

17. **Warm-up and check marks only**

18. **Pool** a. swimming, b. intervals of shallow, c. intervals of deep

M (Same as Sprinters for Warm-Up)
(10 H x 12 with 55 yard walk (Steady Between)
(to Weight Room - All Partner Poly metrics)
(full weight Routine)

Tu (1 to 1320) (2a slow & fast to 40 x 4 ea.)
(8 single leg boxes to 15) (7a (1)(2) x 6 ea.)
(4a x 4 for Time) (4E x 6 full) (RRR -LLL x 6)
Easy Run around JD. Park

W Full warm-up
Trial at 35.2 x 2
full weight Room Routine

Th (1 to 1320) (2a-b-c x 4 ea.)
(5a x 4 Drop Down)
(stretch Out when finished

F (1 to 1320) (2a-b-c x 9ea) (6a x 6)
(7a x 6) (4D (1) x 6 ea leg) (8a x 6)
(100 yds of hopping ea leg x 2) (to weight room

S Easy run to 4-6 miles

166

9. Weights
   a. Special (1) clean & jerk, (2) single leg squats, (3) weighted vest, (4) lead leg drill
   b. Circuit
   c. Power strength (general)

10. Running sets a. 40, b. 50, c. 60, d. 70, e. 80, f. 100, g. 110, h. 165, i. 180, j. 220, k. 330, l. 352, m. 440, n. 500, o. 550, p. 600, q. 880, r. 1000

11. Hurdles (same letters as above)

S Easy Jog or Swim (16)

Comments:

VIKTOR SANEYEV, U.S.S.R.

COPYRIGHT © 1970, PHIL BATH

| 8-1 | 8-2 | 8-3 | 8-4 | 8-5 | 8-6 |

8-7   8-8   8-9   8-10   8-11   8-12

8-18   8-19   8-20   8-21

8-26   8-27   8-28   8-29

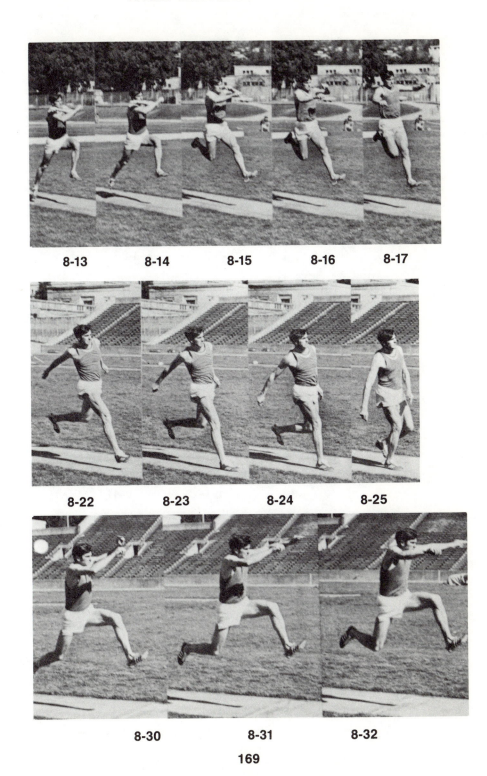

8-13   8-14   8-15   8-16   8-17

8-22   8-23   8-24   8-25

8-30   8-31   8-32

8-33   8-34   8-35

8-39   8-40   8-41

8-45   8-46

8-36   8-37   8-38

8-42   8-43   8-44

8-47

9

The Shot Put

In developing a plan to increase effectiveness in shot putting, one should consider three basic areas of mechanics for the thrower.
- The angle at which the shot is released from the thrower's hand.
- The height at which the implement can be released.
- The speed at which the shot can be released.

The last, that of increasing speed, is the primary area where coaching and training can bring about desired improvements for the athlete. It has been demonstrated that with a thrower showing a constant 7' above-ground release, an angle of projection at 40° and with the shot moving at 42 feet per second, the implement will travel 61'8". However, with the 7' release and 40° again being constant but increasing the speed of release from 42 to 44 feet per second, the shot will travel 67'0". (Naturally we cannot drastically change the height at which an athlete can release the shot as this is determined by the thrower's physical capability.)

The angle of release for maximum distance is always best when the vertical and horizontal components are equal, and when using a trajectory that leaves the ground and returns to the ground, the optimum release angle will always be 45°. It is understood, however, that in throwing events the trajectory never originates on the ground. There-fore the angle of release must be under 45°. It has been determined that angles between 40° and 42° will provide the most desired results.

Some evaluation should be made regarding the angle of release for every thrower. This is easily determined diagramatically in the following manner:

First, plot a vertical line through the shot at the instant of release and then run another line to the point at which the shot lands. The angle of release is then determined by bisecting the two plotted lines (Fig. 9-1).

FIGURE 9-1

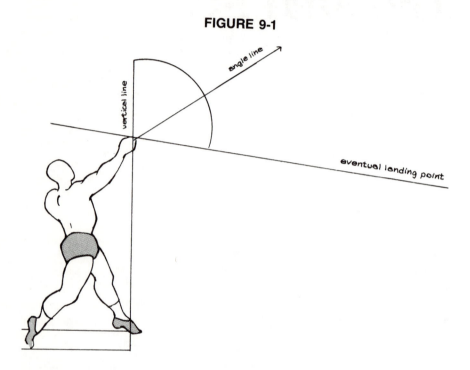

Once the athlete has developed the proper foot base power position, the angle of release will not present a problem. The sequence of events leading to the proper throwing position will be discussed later in detail.

However, it is important to remember that of the three primary concerns—angle, height, and release speed—speed of release is by far the most important. Strength and technique training greatly improve the athlete's ability to put the shot. Specifically, they influence release speed. For this reason strength and technique must comprise the bulk of an athlete's training program.

Perhaps the most important influence on release speed comes from the hinge and pyramid "moment" principle. These block or stop established momentum. It is through these actions that acceleration can be developed. When a body is moving in a straight path and is suddenly checked, angular momentum is developed to all points above the center of gravity.

When a car is moving straight and the car hits a wall, stopping suddenly, the driver is thrown forward. The quicker or more suddenly the car stops, the more the angular momentum is transferred to the driver. When the shot's velocity is established either by the glide or rotation across the circle, and the thrower wishes to utilize the hinged principle, he must quickly check the forward momentum of his feet. The checking action must be sudden and with no dissipation of force (such as the hips and shoulders sliding forward.) If the checking is rapid with no forward sliding of the body, there is a great acceleration to all body parts and implements that are located above the foot fulcrum. This blocking or checking action is probably the most important ingredient in increasing speed of release of the shot.

The pyramid "moment" action is related to the hinge principle but is applied in another manner. This characteristic has to do with developing a foot base preliminary to the throw. Again, the body is divided into segments below and above the center of gravity during rotational movement. If the feet are more than shoulder-width apart during a rotational movement, the speed of all body parts above the center of gravity will increase. This increased speed is transferred to the shot. Inversely, when the foot support base is narrower than shoulder width, there is a decrease of upper body rotational speed. Obviously then, in all throwing events the foot base must be wider than shoulder width.

A third factor necessary for increasing release speed involves additional muscle summation and even the storage of momentum and force. This is described as torque development. Torque, in this event as well as all others, is simply the twisting action between the upper and lower halves of the body. In coaching terminology, "separation of hips and shoulders" is the key to energy storage. Rather than the entire trunk working as a unit, the thrower wishes to lead with the hips, creating a torque between hips and shoulders (Fig. 9-2).

FIGURE 9-2
"Torque" Shoulder Hip Separation

One key to the development of the "torque" position is to allow the knee of the supporting foot to relax or collapse inward. As the knee cannot actually bend in a lateral position, this is accomplished by being high on the toe with the toe inverted inward.

Ground Reaction

In all throwing events (and the shot is no exception) "ground reaction" is a key to the development of effective throwing. Ground reaction has two components—one a vertical direction and the other a horizontal direction. These two determine not only the angle of release but also ground force. According to Newton's Third Law of Motion, for every force an athlete imparts into the ground, a counter force will occur off the ground back into the athlete's body and eventually into the implement.

The two items controlling the amount of ground reaction are strength (which can be developed) and body weight (which can also be developed). A 150 pound athlete exerts 150 pounds of force against the ground and, of course, 150 pounds of force is given back from the ground. Obviously, then, if a thrower weighs 300 pounds, the ground delivers back 300 pounds which is magnified into distance a thrower can deliver an implement. All things being equal, the heavier the athlete, the more force can be applied to the implement.

Basic Steps in Teaching The Shot Put Event

The Grip
The best means of holding the shot is the same used when simply picking the implement up. In doing this, the weight of the shot is distributed throughout the hand, but most importantly it does not rest on the heel of the hand but is forward into the palm. Many throwers like to spread the fingers and others like the fingers all to be touching. The spread position is usually best for beginners as it tends to provide better balance in the hand.

Foot Power Base
Before attempting to establish a (glide or rotation) type of throw, it is a "must" to learn to throw from a standing, proper power position.

Perhaps it is best to instruct the thrower that the delivery occurs from the legs and back. In the early stages of learning very little emphasis is placed on the arm throw. The arm constitutes only a minor amount of force in putting the shot.

The basic power position is a heel-toe foot stance. This is necessary so the weight of the thrower can go up and over the left leg.

The common yet ineffective position of the feet is what we call "in the bucket" stance. This open position of the hips makes it impossible to get weight up over the left leg (Figure 9-4).

It is also undesirable to allow the left foot to be approximately parallel to the right foot as no transference of force can occur.

Experience has shown that an effective way to teach the power foot position is for the young athlete to stand with feet together at right angles to the direction of throw. Then, the athlete steps with the right foot into the power position, rotating so that the back now is pointing in the direction of throw. The weight is directly over a bent right leg with little or no weight over the left foot. In addition, the hips and shoulders are separated to establish the necessary torque of the large back and abdominal muscles. The shoulders should be parallel to the ground. A conscious effort must be made to keep the left and leading shoulder at least as low as the right shoulder. The head is down with the eyes directed to the back of the ring. The left arm should be relaxed and hanging so the hand is even with the toe of the right foot (Fig. 9-3.).

FIGURE 9-3

Power Base Throwing

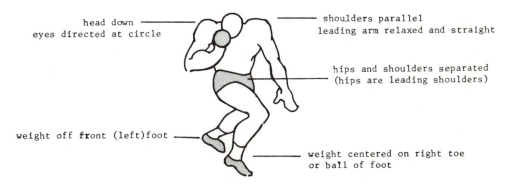

foot base is heel and toe with hips closed

Once the athlete can move into the power position with some proficiency, he or she can begin some easy throwing. However, the emphasis must be on keeping the feet (especially the back foot) on the ground throughout the throw. If the common mistake of throwing with the back foot off the ground occurs, the hips will slide forward and no blocking impulse can be made.

Analysis of "good" shot putters and discus throwers will show that the front foot, near the scratch line, will actually clear the ground before the power back foot. This action not only allows maximum extension of the back leg but causes the hips to stop for an instant. This stopping or blocking action will accelerate the shot as was discussed in the hinge movement principle.

An important body position to note during any throw is the "Backward C Power Point." This position assures that the back and abdominal muscles are being utilized (Fig. 9-5).

FIGURE 9-4

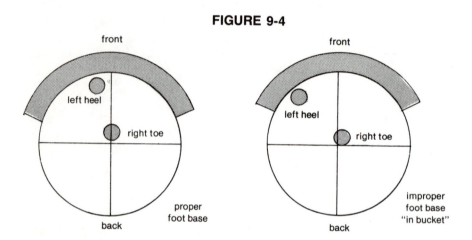

Throwing Actions

Throwing actions although secondary in importance to the feet, hips and trunk, deserve some attention at this time. To begin with, the shot is to be cradled under the chin and in contact with the neck. The ball must never lose contact with the neck until the actual throw begins. The elbow must be kept high throughout the preliminary movements so that the athlete utilizes all the pectoral and anterior deltoid muscles in addition to the triceps muscles. Even more important, however, is keeping the elbow up. This not only elicits power in muscle contractions, but it sets up a coordinated line of direction with the fast moving free and leading arm.

At the instant the shot is released the throwing hand goes into a quick, flexed, outward-blocking action. This is commonly called the "swimming action" of the wrist. The movement is similar to the pulling action of the wrist when swimming the breast stroke. This very important high blocking action creates an equal and opposite reaction with the hips. The faster the arm goes into the block, the faster the hips turn in the opposite direction. The high push allows for full and complete extension of the pushing power leg. This maneuver probably increases by nearly one foot the distance a 16 pound ball can be thrown.

Mention should also be made of the opposite free or swing arm. This not only initiates direction and pull to the chest and putting arm by providing a long inertia breaking lever, but also a short speed lever to the open shoulder position. At the beginning stage, when the thrower is in the power stance position, it has already been indicated that the arm should be extended and relaxed. After the initial rotary motion of the lower body, which through body torque and separation begins the throwing action, the long extended arm generates much force but little speed. That means this free arm will stay extended through most of the rotation movement of the hips and shoulders. However, as the hips and following upper body move into the front throwing position, the leading free arm quickly flexes to 90° and pulls back as forcefully as possible. The shortened lever provides two functions. First, the increased arm speed places great elastic stretch across the entire left shoulder and through the chest, providing greatly magnified muscle contractibility. Secondly, the accelerated movement gives the necessary speed to the opening shoulders prior to the release of the shot (Fig. 9-5).

When maximum speed of the free flexed arm is achieved, the shot will be near the point of release. It is important for the thrower to remember this latter action of the throw is not a power but a speed action. To summarize, the total movement of the glide and throw begin relatively slowly with the larger power areas and finally terminates with the short-levered speed application.

No matter how fast a thrower moves from the glide to the power foot base, it will not aid the actual throw if there is not a continual build-up of speed through the actual release.

The old axiom states force x time = power. Therefore, it must be remembered that the longer the athlete is able to maintain foot contact with the ground, the longer hand contact is possible with the shot. The best throwers maintain contact with the shot well out beyond the board. The farther out, the better in terms of throwing distance.

In learning the "reaching out" technique, one must develop an effective crossover of the feet to prevent fouling or stepping over the toe board. Many fouls can be eliminated by simply lowering the center of gravity, bending down at the knees and hips.

179

FIGURE 9-5

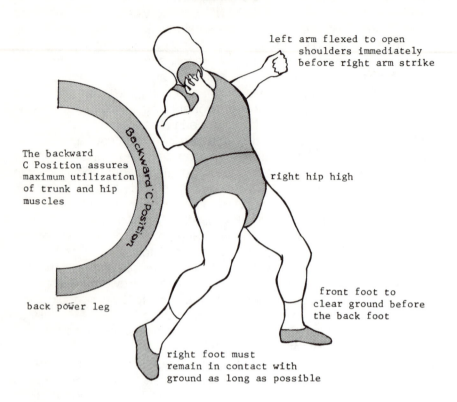

left arm flexed to open
shoulders immediately
before right arm strike

The backward
C Position assures
maximum utilization
of trunk and hip
muscles

Backward "C" Position

right hip high

back power leg

front foot to
clear ground before
the back foot

right foot must
remain in contact with
ground as long as possible

The Glide

The glide is a term that has evolved from the Parry O'Brien technique. Basically it is a preparatory phase which allows momentum to be transferred from preliminary body movements in the back of the circle to the power foot base throwing position. It is a means to break inertia and get the shot moving over a long period of time. It is also used to place the body into torque or shoulder-hip separation. To be effective, a glide must begin gradually with never a delay or stoppage of movement.

It is understood that the glide provides horizontal velocity to the shot but many coaches and throwers overestimate its importance. The expert thrower can expect no more than a 10% distance improvement through a well-initiated glide over his standing throw from the power position.

Not only should the coach be aware of the limitations gained from the glide, but the specific glide technique must be fitted to the individual athlete. The thrower's weight is to be distributed over the toes of the back power foot. Movement or body position of any kind that centers weight ahead of this back foot is unwanted.

Body position or torque built up at the back of the circle (before the athlete reaches the throwing position) will have no effect on the eventual throw. Positive results will occur only when torque is established at the power base position. The key then is to simply develop a glide that allows the athlete to land and continue with no delay into the throw. The actual throw is begun at the instant the back foot comes into contact with the circle. From the glide the foot strike of both feet should be almost simultaneous with the back foot landing slightly before the front. The all-too-common mistake of stopping or delaying movement from the glide to the throw will destroy any advantage the back ring motion has developed.

Rotation Style of Putting

With the advent of many world class athletes using a rotational or discus style of shot putting, some mention must be directed to that technique. It should be remembered that the rotational technique is really nothing more than a means of placing the shot into motion before reaching our already-described power base position.

The rotational thrower still must spend considerable time working and developing the power foot, leg, hip and shoulder technique.

The rotational technique actually is a trade-off for the conventional glide preparation. It has some advantages and some disadvantages. The primary advantage of this style of throw preparation is the extra distance in which the shot can accelerate. However, increased distance is at the expense of straight line movement and, perhaps more importantly, balance. It is difficult to rotate and keep the necessary wide foot placement and the required hip and shoulder separation maintained.

It should be noted, however, that in spite of the deviation from the straight line when using the glide style, the rotation has greater potential for maximum shot acceleration. Therefore, used properly, the rotation will increase the velocity of the implement at the release. Remember, the speed of release is the most important ingredient for developing distance in the shot put. This glide style will definitely provide an advantage to the smaller and quicker athletes.

The following is a summary of technique designed especially for the rotation type of throw.

Basic Objectives to be Developed
for Rotation Shot Putting Style

1. Develop a perfect pivot.
2. Maintain balance throughout the turn and into the throwing position.
3. Accurate foot placement (power foot base) for effective power position.

4. Directional control.
5. Attempt to lead into the turn with the lower body and not the shot.

Problems Which Occur and Are Unique to the Rotational Thrower

1. Centrifugal force always requires a counteracting force; therefore, weight must be centered directly over the pivot foot.
2. Difficulty in keeping the shot under the chin; rotational force is primarily developed around the implement.
3. Difficulty of reaching an exact point from which the shot can be *delivered in a straight line* after circular acceleration.
4. The feet usually stabilize in **too narrow** a base of support for an effective throw.
5. The body tends to continue turning during the delivery. The opposite shoulder cannot be "posted" or fixed. It tends to continue rotating. The same problem is apparent in the hips. To develop torque, hips, too, must be stopped in delivery.
6. The "big advantage" of acceleration is lost many times when the left foot is brought down too late. This action destroys the long *acceleration phase.*
7. Because of the rotational force it is difficult to get "reach" (maintaining contact with the shot until it is well out beyond the front foot). Correction here can only come about by landing in a good, wide-base throwing position.
8. Rotational force will cause the athlete to shorten the distance the shot is moved from the putting stance to the moment of release. Again, only through a conscious effort to lengthen distance of force application can acceleration be achieved.

General Skills to be Developed

1. Assume stance slightly to the right of the circle. This helps the necessary quick *short* sprint step to the front of the circle. Remain erect during the turn, keeping weight directly over pivot point. Squat during the turn and remain low, but keep shoulders perpendicular.
2. Start movement rather slowly as the shot will immediately gain speed and "runs light" throughout the turn. It is difficult for the body to keep up. Also, start movement with a wide base support—slightly wider than shoulders allows a pyramid action of acceleration and torque development.
3. Execute the turn as in the discus.
4. Land from the turn in the throwing position. *Do not* allow the left foot to loop around. The foot must be brought through in a straight down movement, not circular. A good drill is front sprinting; run into back of the circle facing the direction of the throw, then perform

a quick turn landing into the throwing position. Quick rotation of the hips.

5. Always check the reach at the release of the shot. In a good throw the hand is in contact with the shot well beyond the fulcrum front foot.

6. Check hip shoulder separation at the instant of landing in the throwing position.

7. Check for the in-the-bucket position. The left foot should never go beyond the center line of the ring.

8. Check the length of delivery force upon reaching the throwing position. Too short (less than approximately 4 feet) will mean the foot base is too narrow.

9. Always delay hip rotation prior to actual release. A problem here usually occurs when base of support is too narrow.

10. Just prior to the release the hips must be posted or stopped to insure added acceleration to the striking arm.

11. Never allow the arm to start delivery until the front foot has been planted.

WEEKLY WORKOUT
for
Shot & Discus Throwers

NAME: **DATE:** 10 / 16 / 82

1. **Easy jogging**

2. **Full stretching warm-up**

3. **Sprint accelerations to 70 yds.**

4. **Weight training**
   a. Circuit training
   b. Power strength
   c. Special lifts

5. **Depth jumping**
   a. Step off box; jump as high as possible (single & double leg)
   b. 40" to 18" to ground to 18"
   c. Hop from 18" box into shot power position with shot

6. **Power exercises for legs**
   a. Hurdle hopping
   b. Double leg hops up stairs
   c. Double leg hops down stairs
   d. Single leg hops up stairs

13. **See coach** (a) film study (b) pictures

14. **Full warm-up & stretch out throwing**

15. **Pool** (a) swimming (b) intervals shallow (c) intervals deep

M (1 to ½ mile)(2×15 min.)
(6a×15)(6B×6)(5A×15)
(4 3 full)

T (1 to ½ mile)(2×15 min)
(12 Stand × 10 min.)(12 full glide × 10 min)
(12×6 full effort)(2 full)(cool down)

W (1 to ½ mile)(2×15 min.)
6a × 15)(7a × 25 × 2 sets)(3×4)
(9B × 12)(Standing long jumps × 15)
(4B full)

183

7. Medicine ball drills
    a. Two handed over head forward from behind head (knees)
    b. Putting with right arm
    c. Baseball throw with right arm
    d. Two handed chest pass
    e. Throw forward from between legs

8. Running
    a. Squat hop sprints (40-50 m)
    b. Bounding sprint
    c. Sprints from starting blocks
    d. Interval training

9. Agility drills
    a. Bench hopping
    b. Carioka running 5-10x40-50 yds.
    c. Lateral line drills
    d. Stretch turn leaps from a squatting position jump into the air making 360°
    e. Turn leaps over low hurdle
    f. Run intermediate hurdles

10. Negative resistance
    a. Overweight incline press
    b. Shot & discus incline

11. Hungarian leg-power speed
    a. Half jump squats b. half jump squats
    c. Hopping backward on power leg
    d. Fast leg drills
    e. Standing long jumps
    f. Backward standing long jumps

12. Throwing drills (a) scaling & South African (b) Dry throwing (c) overweight implements (d) underweight implements (e) standing throw (f) full form throw

T (1 to ½ mile) (2x15min.) (12 B x6) (12 F until fatigue) (with towel) (4 x Stadium Stair sprints)

F Max. Weight Test Preceed with full Warm-Up Swimming - Cool Down

S Your choice

S Your choice

Weight:
Comments:

AL FEUERBACH, U.S.A.

9-1   9-2   9-3

9-4   9-5   9-6

9-7   9-8   9-9

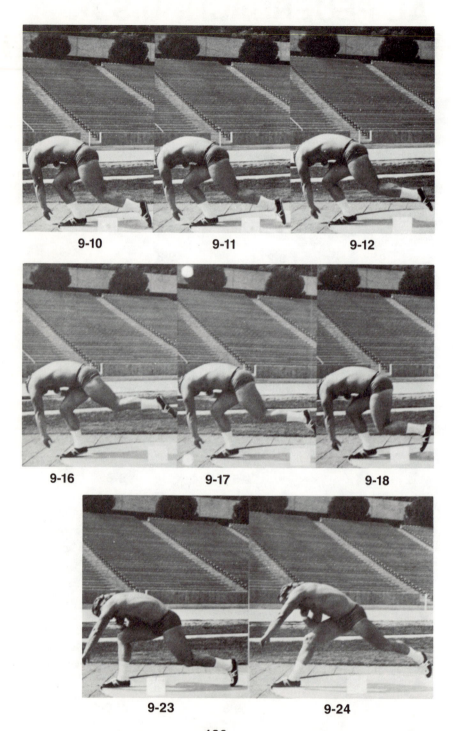

9-10 9-11 9-12

9-16 9-17 9-18

9-23 9-24

9-13 9-14 9-15

9-19 9-20 9-21 9-22

9-25 9-26

9-27   9-28

9-31   9-32

9-29   9-30

9-33   9-34   9-35

9-36   9-37   9-38

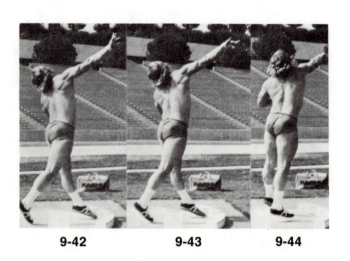

9-42   9-43   9-44

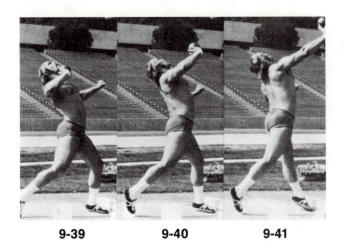

9-39   **9-40**   **9-41**

9-45   **9-46**

10

The Discus

Since the discus is affected by lift principles in the same manner as an airplane wing, it can be considered an airfoil. The phenomenon of lift may be explained as follows: as air velocity increases over the top surface of an airfoil, an inverse increase of upward pressure beneath the airfoil will cause it to lift.

In relating this lift to the discus, you must consider four factors:
1. velocity,
2. angle of attack,
3. angle of projection, and
4. rotation.

Velocity is developed through various muscular contractions. The various principles of physics involved in the mechanics of the actual throw will be discussed later.

The angle of attack can be described as the tilting upwards of the discus in flight. Ganslen's studies, *Aerodynamic and Mechanical Forces in discus flight,* and Bunn's book *Scientific Principles of Coaching* indicate that the ideal angle of projection (the angle in which the implement is released in relation to the ground) is approximately 35° and the angle of attack is near 25.°

The combination of these two angles seems to give optimum results whenever the velocity is from 75 to 80 feet per second. Ganslen describes this as the average velocity developed by a discus thrower. When the angle of attack exceeds 26° to 29,° the discus tends to stall and lose its lifting qualities. At this point, only the initial velocity created by muscular force carries the discus.

In treating the measurements of the aforementioned angles, the coach must obtain the assistance of a stop-action motion picture and project the sequence on a lined grid screen. The angle measurements can be made with a protractor.

The third factor—rotation—is often neglected by coaches and athletes. Rotation has to do with gyroscopic force—the clockwise turning of the discus. The spin has a stabilizing effect which tends to hold the discus on course and steady it throughout flight. Motion picture studies indicate that a discus will revolve from five to eight revolutions per second during flight.

When visualizing this turning in flight, it must be understood that the speed of the discus on the left leading side will be greater than the speed on the right side, causing greater lift on the left side. This factor must be dealt with in relation to the hand angle (inward or outward rotation and slight flexion or hyper-extension) at the point of release, especially when dealing with wind angles.

Effects of Wind on Discus Throwing

It's generally understood that a head wind is beneficial to discus throwing, whereas a tail wind, although adding impetus to the implement, is detrimental to the throw.

The primary factor with regard to head wind is that the added wind velocity coming over the leading edge of the discus increases the lifting effect. This permits the implement to be released at a lesser angle, thereby causing less air resistance and drag. Thus, less velocity is necessary to carry the discus.

All the research into wind effects substantiate the fact that the best angle of release is approximately 25° when throwing into a head wind whose velocity is less than 14 miles per hour. It has also been established that a head wind of seven to eight miles per hour produces optimum results.

When the head wind exceeds 14½ miles per hour, it usually hinders the discus throw. Though the lifting effect is increased, the added wind resistance distinctly reduces the distance covered.

The presence of a tail wind greatly decreases the lifting effect because of the loss of wind velocity over the lead edge of the discus. Technically speaking, the vacuum centered about the trailing edge of the discus is greatly reduced, in contrast to the desirable vacuum tail suction produced by throwing into a wind.

The athlete who must throw into an excessive head wind would do best by throwing across the wind. If possible, the discus circle should be set up so the wind blows slightly from right to left. You never want to have the wind approaching from left to right. Because of the superior lifting capabilities of the left side of the discus, the left-to-right wind would magnify the possibilities of the discus turning over in flight.

Procedure and Analysis of the Throw

Before the actual throw, all body manipulations should be aimed at developing linear velocity through speed, rotary motion, torque, and friction. The thrower must operate from a circle measuring 8'2½" across. If there was limitless space from which to operate, the distances would undoubtedly be greatly improved.

In determining the most efficient body positioning and movements, the thrower must consider several factors: he must take advantage of all distance possible in the ring, and he must generate as much speed as possible before the actual release.

The speed must be controlled for balance, or center-of-gravity placement. This leads to the question, "Should the thrower revolve from one turn, one and one-half turns, or one and three-quarter turns?"

The determining factor is body type. For example, a smaller and more coordinated man will move faster and be under greater control (because his center of gravity will be lower) than a larger, slower athlete. Since the smaller man's leverage isn't as great as the larger man's, speed must compensate for leverage, or vice versa.

It is, therefore, essential to study the individual's body type before committing him to a definite style. In general, we'd want the athlete to take a relaxed standing position, somewhere within 180 to 205° of a line perpendicular to the direction of the throw. The entire turn will go through approximately 520.

The weight should be evenly distributed over both feet to begin the preparatory swings. At this point, the thrower should be completely relaxed and concentrating fully on the throw itself. Any undue tension will affect the preliminary swing, especially. The primary function of this swing is to bring the discus as far behind the shoulder as possible.

After the preparatory swings (usually three), the head should turn clockwise, looking back toward the arm, with the trailing arm and discus back of the shoulder to increase the rotary motion. The turning of the head allows the discus to move back from the shoulder anywhere from 80 to 100,° adding to the range of motion.

As the discus travels back on the final preliminary swing, the body weight, which was equally distributed over both feet, comes over the right knee and foot, and at the same time the left foot goes into an unforced position of plantar flexion.

The amount of backward rotation of the right arm has a direct relationship to knee flexion. The more flexion of the knees (over 90° for the left and somewhat less than that for the right), the farther back the discus can be located beyond the normal line of the shoulders.

During this phase of the turn, many inexperienced throwers allow the left foot to drop back into the circle, assuming this will give them a more balanced position. Actually, this maneuver shortens the distance of the circle, thus handicapping the thrower's velocity and body torque.

The spin is now initiated by locking the right arm in the back position, with the discus being held at near shoulder level. If it is held lower, it will produce too great an angle of release, reducing lift or even causing the discus to turn over in flight.

The body weight must be shifted from the right foot onto the ball and toes of the left foot. The thrower should never touch the heel to the ground at any point in the turn. The leading right leg must now begin to come around and across the left.

Most discus throwers lead slightly with the knee, then assume what appears to be a sprint position as they come out of the turn. At this point, the main effort is directed toward torque development, balance, and speed.

Torque or body separation, a force capable of producing a power rotation of the body, is established by several actions. The trail arm is located behind the shoulder with the elbow completely extended, thus increasing the line of pull and decelerating the upper body during the turn. Conversely, the lower body, with the lead leg extended and moving fast, develops a twisting tendency between the lower and upper body.

This contributes to the idea of leading with the foot on the turn. In the past years, however, Utah State athletes, including Jay Silvester and Glen Passey, have used with great success the principle of leading with a straight leg on the cross-over at the beginning of the turn. Modifications of this action have recently been used by Mac Wilkins, Al Oerter and John Powell, with good results.

The straight leg tends to open the thighs and produce a larger amount of angular momentum, yielding more speed. In addition there is a high degree of torque that develops between the lower and upper body, thus storing energy until the power-throwing position is reached. In addition, the thrower will eliminate turning with the hop, and putting themselves back on the ground faster with a snapping, explosive movement.

Another important factor is keeping the right heel high in the first step of the turn. Although the good thrower will want to land with the right foot in an inwardly rotated position ahead of the body, many throwers come around on the turn, placing the foot down first and then making the rotation on the ground. By turning the foot in the air and bringing it to the ground ready to throw, the thrower will not only effect a rotation in the hips but will carry it on down into the rotating foot and toes, consequently developing much greater force.

When the heel is held high in the turn, it automatically lands in a correct position. If the athlete shows no concern for the high heel position, he'll find it exceedingly difficult to develop this rotation simply by turning in the foot prior to landing.

Al Oerter, in his later years, used this skill well. However, most throwers land with the pivoting toe pointed toward the back of the ring. This is the case with Jay Silvester (photos 10-19, 10-20, 10-21).

The thrower should make all contact (foot placement) in a line. A straight-line approach is the most effective in providing distance and power through the circle. Therefore, as the athlete comes around on the first turn, he should touch the right foot down on a line bisecting the ring perpendicular to the line of throw.

The trailing or swinging leg is brought around wide to a point where the knee passes the hips (Silvester, photos 10-10, 10-16). The athlete now wants to "spring" through and cut down as quickly as possible. The key here, however, is to drive off the back foot (keeping it on the ground as long as possible). The thrower in essence sprints and cuts down on a straight line across the circle.

It's desirable to plant the feet in the "power base position" described in Chapter 9, Figure 4. The main objective is to keep a wide and stable base. The foot base must be at least shoulder width, and usually slightly wider. The wide base is the only means to achieve a quick stopping or braking action. The "brake" is absolutely necessary to establish the hinge moment between the lower and upper body. The faster the lower body stops, the faster the upper body and the discus accelerate.

The left leg must be brought back as quickly as possible and land close to the scratch line, just off to the left of the throwing direction. Its primary function is to serve as a brake (hinge movement) and to transfer all rotary motion to linear motion. The more efficient this transfer of energy, the greater the velocity of the discus in flight.

This means that no matter how much speed and power are developed, the motion transfer from one direction to another must be simultaneous and smooth, or most of the effort in the turn will be lost. This trail leg must come around quickly and begin the extension of the knee as the body weight passes over it, thus creating the lifting power of the discus.

The leading arm plays an important part in body force and acceleration for releasing stored energy into the throw. In initiating the turn at the back of the circle, the arm swings wide to develop angular momentum. However, as the turn begins, the leading arm is brought in close to the body. This shortening of the radius speeds up the turn. Then when the turn is completed and the long pull begins, the lead arm extends "long and wide" again. This time, however, its function is to place the chest and throwing arm into a stretch for more muscular power. The last action of the lead arm is to block (stop) the forearm in near the body, causing a hinge movement, accelerating the throwing arm and shoulder, (see Silvester, photos 10-30, 10-31).

The athlete is now into position for the final stages of the turn, ready for the actual throw. He or she must consider the angle of the discus in relation to the body for the most efficient release.

Once the feet are planted prior to the throw, the discus follows an interesting path—first declining below the hips, then rapidly coming up to release point just above the level of the shoulder. The angle of the discus in flight stems not so much from hand positioning as from the path the discus follows in relation to the straightening of the left leg and the leveling of the shoulders.

Doherty indicates that to obtain the optimum 30° angle of release, the discus must not be more than six inches below shoulder height with the arm at a right angle to the direction of the throw. But most throwers now feel the release should be just above the shoulder upon release (Silvester, photo 10-33).

As the actual throw is made, both feet should be in contact with the ground. We like to instruct our athletes to actually pull the front foot off the ground before the back foot clears the surface. This guarantees complete extension of the back power foot. This helps secure a simultaneous lift and push (with both legs) in coordination with a forceful contraction of the pectoral and chest area on the right side and the pulling back of the rotator muscles on the left (pulling) side.

After the discus has left the hand, some athletes believe that a forceful closing of the hand will furnish added impetus to the discus. Others feel that a slight dropping of the thumb (pronation) will help flatten the discus and help eliminate a wobbling motion while in flight.

As the discus is released, the thrower begins crossing the right leg over the left on his reverse. To avoid falling over the scratch line, he can bend his legs at the knees and drop his center of gravity.

WEEKLY WORKOUT
for
Shot & Discus Throwers

NAME: DATE:

1. **Easy jogging**

2. **Full stretching warm-up**

3. **Sprint accelerations to 70 yds.**

4. **Weight training**
   a. Circuit training
   b. Power strength
   c. Special lifts

13. **See coach** (a) film study (b) pictures

14. **Full warm-up & stretch out throwing**

15. **Pool** (a) swimming (b) intervals shallow (c) intervals deep

5. Depth jumping
   a. Step off box; jump as high as possible
     (single & double leg)
   b. 40" to 18" to ground to 18"
   c. Hop from 18" box into shot power position
     with shot

6. Power exercises for legs
   a. Hurdle hopping
   b. Double leg hops up stairs
   c. Double leg hops down stairs
   d. Single leg hops up stairs

7. Medicine ball drills
   a. Two handed over head forward from behind
     head (knees)
   b. Putting with right arm
   c. Baseball throw with right arm
   d. Two handed chest pass
   e. Throw forward from between legs

8. Running
   a. Squat hop sprints (40-50 m)
   b. Bounding sprint
   c. Sprints from starting blocks
   d. Interval training

9. Agility drills
   a. Bench hopping
   b. Carioka running 5-10x40-50 yds.
   c. Lateral line drills
   d. Stretch turn leaps from a squatting position
     jump into the air making 360°
   e. Turn leaps over low hurdle
   f. Run intermediate hurdles

10. Negative resistance
   a. Overweight incline press
   b. Shot & discus incline

11. Hungarian leg-power speed
   a. Half jump squats b. half jump squats
   c. Hopping backward on power leg
   d. Fast leg drills
   e. Standing long jumps
   f. Backward standing long jumps

12. Throwing drills (a) scaling & South African
   (b) Dry throwing (c) overweight implements
   (d) underweight implements (e) standing throw
   (f) full form throw

M Easy Running with stretching to follow

T 1-2 Register for Classes
Start Weight Training on Tuesday
4b follow the progression on the charts
Mirror drills in the wt. room

W Team Meeting, 3:00, Varsity Center

1-2
12 (spend a lot of time on drills only,
minimum throwing only, Easy run to fol'xul

T 1-2
12 b,e,f
4b light session in the wt. room

F Eligibility meeting at 3:30 in the
Varsity Center, with Lyle Smith
Directly following the meeting, check
out gear from Mel
Light warm-up to follow

S Depart Varsity Center at 7:00 a.m.
for Pocatello
Compete at 1:30
Leave for Boise directly after eating
dinner.

S This week is going to be rather easy,
so make work-out quality with film
study and lots of drill work.
Phinney, start working hard on the
discus.

Weight:
Comments:

JAY SILVESTER, U.S.A.

10-1   10-2   10-3

10-7   10-8   10-9

10-13   10-14   10-15

10-4   **10-5**   **10-6**

10-10   **10-11**   **10-12**

10-16   **10-17**   **10-18**

10-19   **10-20**   **10-21**

10-25   **10-26**   **10-27**   **10-28**

10-32   **10-33**   **10-34**

10-22   **10-23**   **10-24**

10-29   **10-30**   **10-31**

10-35   **10-36**   **10-37**

11

Javelin Technique

Prior to investigating the actual techniques of a javelin thrower it may be well to establish principles to determine distance when throwing the javelin. Those principles are:
- Height above the ground at which the javelin is released.
- Aerodynamics of the javelin and the angles of projection and attack.
- Velocity at the time of release.

The last item, velocity at the time of release, is complicated. Release speed is determined by several factors which include: speed of the run-up and how well this speed can be projected into the throw; the forces and torque which can be built up at the time of release; and finally, the rotation of body parts and the application of the hinge principle and the serape effect of muscular contraction.

Speed of the Run

This provides the first opportunity to initiate speed to the javelin release. The run-up must be as fast as can offer a smooth transition into the setting position and finally the actual throwing movement. As we can see in any running event, effective speed is accompanied by a counter action of the leg and arm movements. The simple act of holding the javelin during the run-up complicates the athlete's ability to coordinate arm and leg movement.

The basic concern in developing a run-up is to keep the hips from twisting away from the straight ahead running direction. The shoulders must remain perpendicular to the runway. The wrist on the javelin must be relaxed and the hand should be allowed to gain a slight pumping action to permit full freedom of the total running action. On the runway, the coach must observe the rear leg kickup of the athlete. The foot during the swing phase must go through a high recovery up near the buttocks. Too many times a runner carrying an implement attempts to run somewhat stiff legged. A true sprint action is what the javelin thrower seeks in an effective run-up.

The most effective length of run seems to be around 13 to 21 strides (total run, including a five step setting and throwing phase). Only 9-13 steps are used to initiate the speed of the run, the remaining 4-8 steps are used in transition—but the key is to maintain momentum. We like to tell our throwers to accelerate through the transition stage, but I doubt this actually occurs.

Throughout the approach and cross over (power step), the athlete must remember that speed is important but the main concern is the velocity of the run-up—primarily to increase torque of the hips and the shoulders. In addition, it sets the body for ultimate usage of the hinge principle and the twisting serape effect of the oblique muscles of the back and abdominal area. These two concerns will be dealt with separately.

Styles of Throws

Most successful throwers by today's standards utilize some modification of the Finnish style. The initiation of the method allows the upper body to get well behind the support of the planting foot, thus giving the thrower the advantage of a long time pull period (see Kinnunen, photos 11-12, 11-13, 11-14, 11-15).

The basic technique employed to *Set* the thrower is provided by what the "old timers" call a front cross over step. The cross over step allows the hips to sink low with the weight centered over the back foot (right leg for a right handed thrower). The weight-supporting knee goes into a 60-65° flexion and the trunk is bent back away from the throwing direction. This flex power set allows the right arm to reach the desired long pulling position.

The following is a step counting technique for learning the Finnish "soft step" cross-over:
1. After the initial speed run-up, the left foot strikes a check mark and the javelin is drawn back with an extended arm-hand set at least level to the shoulder. (The thrower is to run out from under the implement.)
2. The right foot toes out slightly, preferably to 30°.
3. The left foot turns in slightly 25-30° toward the throwing arm.
4. The right foot crosses in front of the left and both feet become airborne. (This is the penultimate stride which sets up the double hinge moment.)

5. The left foot moves one quick long stride forward and is planted heel first and the javelin is delivered.

The foot pattern of the original Finnish Method appears as (Fig. 11-1).

The big draw back of this style of approach is that when the lean back position is achieved, the hips are no longer facing forward and are sideways (they remain parallel to the upper body). This total alignment of the upper and lower body will not allow separation of the shoulders and hips (torque). In addition there is a negative effect on the running ability as the athlete is forced to run with both feet toed out away from the direction of the run. Certainly the above style is inefficient for at least two of our three original objectives of developing speed of release, omit speed of the run-up and force from muscular contractions.

FIGURE 11-1
Foot Pattern of Original Finnish Method

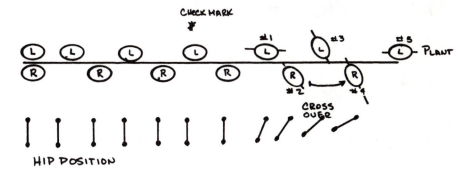

The advantage of the modified European style is to allow maximum speed down the runway (Fig. 11-2). It is accomplished by keeping the feet pointed in the direction of the runway without turning them out toward the side of the throwing arm. The hips, however, are allowed to open slightly on the number one step, but when the right foot is in the air (#4 step) it quickly closes the hips before the foot actually contacts the ground. The true cross over step as it was learned in the Finnish style is impossible to attain in the effective foot ahead position when the hips are closed (as they should be). Instead, this step becomes a high drive power step which not only allows the upper body to come back but also allows for acceleration of the upper body and javelin during the first stage of delivery.

FIGURE 11-2
Modified Finnish or European Style Approach

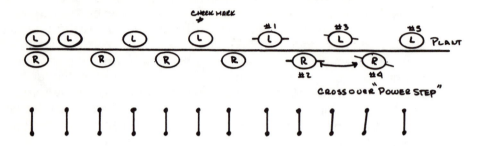

The Double Hinge Principle

The term "hinge principle" or "hinge moment" is used frequently throughout this text, but to summarize, we want the thrower to check linear movement adequately. When an athlete is moving in a straight line and the lower extremity is quickly checked or stopped, angular momentum accelerates any portion of the body above that stopping point. The pole vaulter planting his pole is a classic example. The low portion of the pole is suddenly stopped and the upper portion of the pole accelerates. Fiber glass poles are capable of storing some of this momentum, but the old time steel poles simply changed speed at the two ends.

In the javelin run-up immediately after the front cross over, both feet should be airborne and ahead of the remainder of the body. This sets up the double hinge (see Fig. 11-3, and Kinnunen photos, 11-9, 11-10).

The Serape Effect

To the layman a serape is a blanket worn hanging over the shoulders and lying diagonally over the anterior and posterior portion of the wearer's trunk. The serape muscles include the rhomboids, serratus anterior, external obliques and the internal obliques. These muscles cause oblique and diagonal movements with the pelvic girdle. For a javelin thrower it simply means the timing of movements and speed to bring about the muscle summation of this rotating group of muscles.

Momentum transferred through body position and muscle stretch becomes very useful when weight bearing occurs and the thrower sets up for delivery.

208

FIGURE 11-3

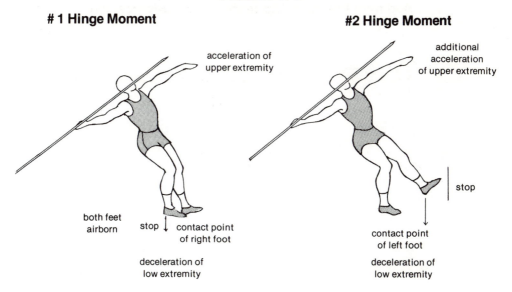

 # 1 Hinge Moment

acceleration of
upper extremity

both feet
airborn   stop ↓ contact point
of right foot

deceleration of
low extremity

#2 Hinge Moment

additional
acceleration
of upper extremity

stop

contact point
of left foot

deceleration of
low extremity

Automatically (if the thrower is in the proper position), body parts begin to rotate forward beginning with the hip and going out through the wrist at release. These actions are given considerably more force and speed when applied through a torqued or separated position of the hips and the shoulders.

The serape effect is developed throughout the checking of linear velocity. At this time momentum is stored in the trunk as the athlete achieves the desired low hip and backward C position, the closed hips and an outward rotation of the back and shoulders (Fig. 11-4).

To summarize the effective throw, the coach and athlete must analyze individually the numerous aspects of the total skill. This is best accomplished by categorizing, step-by-step, the elements of the event.

Grip and Position

The javelin should be held so that it lies diagonally across the hand, with the shaft parallel to the underside of the forearm. The first or second finger should be placed around the shaft. The javelin should be held firmly, with a straight but relaxed wrist (Fig. 11-5).

Preparation to Throw Check-List

1. Establish a desired javelin position at least two steps before the power and cross over steps.

FIGURE 11-4
Going from the Open Hip to the Closed Hip Position

2. Arm should be extended and the hand should be at least shoulder high.
3. Maintain the alignment and angle of the javelin throughout the power step and into the actual throw. The athlete must throw through the tip and not the tail of the javelin.
4. The foot alignment must be in line with the run.
5. DO NOT ALLOW THE FEET TO LAND AND RELAX. THE THROWER MUST POWER THROUGH THE LANDING PHASES.
6. During and after the power step (cross over) the hips should quickly begin to close and square-up with the toeboard.
7. The shoulders must be kept parallel with the javelin. This allows for torque between the shoulders and the hips.
8. The left arm should be held across the chest. This keeps the shoulders from opening up before the planting foot lands.

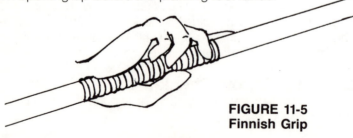

FIGURE 11-5
Finnish Grip

Delivery Check-List

1. At the time of release the body weight should be well back over a flexed right leg at an approximate angle of 60.°
2. The javelin must be pointed in a direct trajectory line of flight.
3. The power or back foot pushes, then stays in contact with the ground. This keeps the hips down until the last moment.
4. The follow through must be up and then over the left leg.
5. The left arm should lead the throw, then during the throw, the left arm is drawn down in the opposite direction to the right throwing arm.
6. Rotate the hips.

WEEKLY WORKOUT FOR JAVELIN

NAME: De Mers   **DATE:** Dec. 1, 1980

Workout	Handwritten notes
1. **Easy jogging** ¼ - ½ mile	**M** (1 to 2 miles) (2) Throwing with Pins Indoors then work with Sprinters (weight)
2. **Full stretching warm-up** (10 min.)	
3. **Spring accelerating** to 70 yds.	
4. **Weight training** a. Circuit training b. Power strength c. Special lifts	**Tu** (1 to 2 miles) (2) Throwing with stubbies (8a × 20, 8b × 2, 8c × 2) (6a × 10) (10b .10min)
5. **Depth jumping** 24″, 40″, 18″ a. Jump off box (40″); jump as high as possible (single and double) b. Jump off box (40″) to 18″ box to ground then jump as high as possible c. Jump from ground to 40″ box to ground then as high as possible	**W** See Me (weights)
6. **Power exercises for legs** a. Hurdle hopping b. Double leg hops up stairs c. Double leg hops down stairs d. Single leg hops up stairs e. Single leg hops down stairs f. Squat thrusts with weight belt	**Th** Same as Sprinters Throwing with Stubbies Indoors 30 minutes - 5 from 24 × 15
7. **Implement throwing** a. Stubby javelins into net b. 8 pound shot—baseball throw from shot ring c. Softball throw Medicine ball a. Two handed overhead—lead with left leg b. Sling throw—two hands underhanded c. Two handed overhead—on knees	**F** 4 × Hill Sprints with Sprinters (weights at Night)

9. **Running**
   a. Bounding sprints
   b. 40 yd. sprints

10. **Agility drills**
    a. Bench hopping
    b. Carioka running
    c. Stretch turn leaps from squatting positions
    d. Intermediate hurdles

11. **Throwing technique**
    a. Sticking—5 to 10 yards for 15 min.
    b. Steps—½ to ¾ effort 15-20 throws
    c. Full approach 10-15 throws

12. **Warm down**—easy jog & walk ½ mile

13. **Warm-up & stretchout throws**

14. **See coach** a. film study   b. pictures

15. **Pool** a. swimming   b. shallow intervals
        c. deep intervals

S *Same as Sprinters*

S

Weight:
Comments:

212

JORMA KINNUNEN, FINLAND

11-1   11-2   11-3

11-4   11-5   11-6

11-7   11-8   11-9

11-10   **11-11**   **11-12**

11-16   **11-17**   **11-18**

11-22   **11-23**

11-13   **11-14**   **11-15**

11-19   **11-20**   **11-21**

11-24   **11- 25**

12

Pole Vault

The mechanics of the pole vault, appear to be complex, but can and should be simplified for the coach and the athlete. Many times the basic points of vaulting have been lost in the shuffle of biomechanical research. Perhaps it is better to concentrate on and develop individual skill objectives. Success in pole vaulting is dependent not only on the athlete but also on the action of the pole. In fact, we consider the pole vault a double pendulum action—the athlete being one pendulum and the pole being the other.

Individual goals for the coach and athlete to concentrate on consist of: speed down the runway, the ability of the athlete to hold high on the pole, penetration (energy into the pole) and angular momentum of the athlete on the pole.

The Runway

As in all running field events, the speed of the athlete will drastically influence the eventual outcome of the performance. Specifically, the faster the athlete, the better the pole vaulting potential. The greater the speed at take-off, the greater will be the response of the pole as it returns energy to the vault. However, upon examination of past champion vaulters, excellent sprint speed is seldom found. From a survey study of top American vaulters, sprint speeds ranged from the best of 9.7

to 10.9 over 100 yards. Although the athlete may not always be blessed with great speed, they must get the best possible momentum out of the run-up and plant. This is the key—to use as much innate speed as is possible.

Runway length will vary from vaulter to vaulter, but usually falls into the range of 110 feet to 150 feet. The exact distance is determined by the ability of the athlete to accelerate to full speed. That means, the faster the athlete, the longer the runway and the slower the athlete, the shorter the runway. A slow athlete will reach top speed much faster than the high speed athlete.

The goal of all vaulters is to develop the skill or capability of planting the pole while running at top speed.

Discussed earlier in detail (in sections on the triple and long jump run-ups) was the idea of little value placed upon a precise distance of approach but of great value on the number of strides on the runway. This is still true in the pole vault. Most important is the number of strides on the runway prior to the actual pole plant.

It is very helpful for the vaulter to begin a season's preparation with a shorter approach to where the plant actually occurs and less than full speed (number of strides). The athlete should gradually lengthen the approach (number of strides) as the season progresses.

Stride counting during the vault approach will tell the athlete where he is on the runway. Through concentrated practice, the vaulter is able to identify the exact drive and plant sequences. Bill Falk talks of the vault being a succession of events happening, each of which is dependent upon the preceding event. Loss or ineffectiveness of any part of the sequence will destroy the final product. By counting the plant foot from the start to the plant, a sequence of events is established and, most importantly, any sequence can be patterned through a progressive step counting. A rhythm or flow on the runway is developed by a count method. The athlete on the runway counts "1"-"2"-"3"-, etc., every time his take-off foot strikes the ground. A jumper who takes 18 total strides during a normal run-up would be counting 9 plant strides.

To develop a runway approach, a vaulter should determine a take-off point by placing the pole in the box, assume the plant position (see proper plant position later in chapter); mark this spot on the runway, then turn and face the opposite direction. The athlete must place the take-off foot on that mark, then begin to run in the opposite direction, counting the plant foot each time it strikes the ground. The coach or another athlete should mark a pre-determined stride number on the runway. After several tries, a consistent mark should be hit on the far end of the runway. Simply reverse the procedure facing the pit and the runway is established from any number of plant foot strides.

Investigation has shown that choice of pole carriage will influence the speed a vaulter can develop down the runway by as much as 0.1

of a second per 50 feet of runway. Therefore, the athlete should select a running style and pole carrying technique that is as close as possible to his normal sprint running style. In the initial part of the run-up, the pole tip should be well above the head. The purpose here is to create a small angle between the pole and the support fulcrum of the hands of the vaulter. this provides a common center of gravity of the pole and the athlete. In essence, this makes the weight of the pole lighter.

However, after the vaulter begins to accelerate away from the first few steps, the pole tip will lower slightly and will remain at eye level throughout the remainder of the run. The height of the pole and carry are extremely important as they allow not only an effective run but are also the forces actively moving the pole forward at the plant. The back hand must not grip the pole as one would hold a baseball bat (Fig. 12-1a). Rather, the index finger should lie along and extend up the shaft of the pole (Fig. 12-1B). This hand should never be allowed to move lower than the top of the hip (illium) throughout the entire run-up or plant.

The front hand is considered the fulcrum and an effective fulcrum must be a solid support. The pole lies between the index finger and the thumb (Fig. 12-1-C). The wrist must remain somewhat extended with the knuckles on the fingers up. This upward alignment of the fingers will allow the wrist to remain under the pole. The general problem of allowing the elbow to collapse during the plant is really caused by the wrist rather than the elbow.

General Faults of the Runway Approach
- Allowing the pole to move forward and backward during the run.
- Slowing down or settling onto the heels going into final plant phase.
- Stopping at the plant and not running through the box.
- Allowing the pole tip to drop lower than eye level.
- Allowing the shoulders to turn out of the straight ahead run-up.
- The back hand "choking" the pole with the palm up.
- The front hand not being in alignment with the shoulder of the back arm.
- Before or during the plant the front arm drops. If the arm drops, so will the knees.

The Plant

The plant is the single most important aspect of the total vault. Remember, however, that the pole plant is completely dependent upon a good run-up, that uses all possible speed.

EFFECTIVE POLE CARRY

FIGURE 12-1A
Ineffective Back Hand

FIGURE 12-1B
Effective Back Hand:
Index Finger Runs Along
Shaft of Pole

FIGURE 12-1C
"High Tip"
Index Finger-Thumb Across
Chest of Front Arm

Perhaps 80% of all work should be devoted to the development of a good plant. Usually the problems occurring in the air are either directly or indirectly related to a problem occurring during the plant.

The key item to remember is the need for *maintaining* horizontal velocity during the run-up. In general, to be effective, the plant should be early, high and directly over the head with the arms pushing through the pole. The early plant is initiated within the last three running strides (the second to the last count step) before the actual plant. If the vaulter has an eight-count stride approach, he will initiate the plant on number seven. Only from an early plant can a vaulter "punch" energy into the pole. The high plant will allow ease of the pole bend. The direct alignment over the head keeps all the forces in a straight-line-run action off the ground.

Vaulters use a variety of pole plants, most of which fall into one of two categories, the side arm curl and the overhand.

The side arm curl plant is used by many vaulters regardless of its many inefficiencies. The top arm is curled as with a bicep curl and weight. The hand will usually travel wide and away from the hip.

Only if the athlete is able to keep the top hand close to the hip can the plant be effective. If the curl is wide and away from the hip (as it usually is), the pole *cannot* get into a high, over-the-head, square position. Consequently, not only will the vaulter be off balance, but the plant will always be late.

The overhand method, although similar to the side arm curl, is by far the most effective style to learn and develop. Rather than a curl action, it resembles a forward "uppercut" action. The top hand moves more in a frontal direction and thus will stay in close to the hip (Fig. 12-2a). The overhand is performed in *front* of the vertical plane of the body. This forward action occurs in the following manner: the back hand moves from its original position at the top of the hip to a forward "uppercut" at the level of the ear, then immediately pushes *through* the pole (Fig. 12-2b). This push action must be initiated with both hands at the instant the pole tip contacts the stop board. Both hands should be moving forward with the left arm blocking but not locking at the elbow.

As the vaulter counts the next-to-the-last "count step," the top hand moves forward to the hip and upward to the level of the ear. By the time the athlete moves to the last running stride, both arms should be fully extended, ready to exert force forward and upward through the pole (Fig. 12-2c).

Up until 1980, athletes had been taught to plant high with the top hand directly in line with the heel of the take-off foot (Fig. 12-3). This characteristic plant style is now undergoing some adjustment as we study a few of the best Americans and most of the good European plant techniques. The tendencies developed by these great vaulters are toward a more forward position of the upper hand (Fig. 12-4). The primary

THE OVERHAND PLANT

FIGURE 12-2A

FIGURE 12-2B

FIGURE 12-2C

Photos by Chuck Sheer

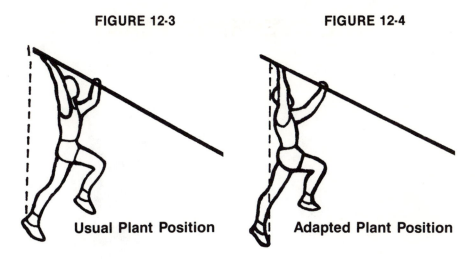

FIGURE 12-3

FIGURE 12-4

Usual Plant Position

Adapted Plant Position

advantage of this plant position is the ability to keep the body away from the pole. It should be noted, however, that much more drive is necessary to reach this particular plant position. Regardless of the plant position used, it is absolutely necessary that the pole be high over the head and in a runway edge of the box before the plant foot hits the ground.

Blow Box Drill

Too many times a beginning vaulter assumes the pole to be the key to successful bar clearance. This, along with a fearful hesitation to drive through the plant, causes many improper technique habits when vaulting into a fixed box. Therefore, every vaulter from the beginner to the advanced should take advantage of runway and planting drills, those individual skills which, where "part" skills are when perfected, make the total vault successful.

Perhaps the most important drill in developing the vault is the runway plant into a sliding box drill in which the vaulter need not leave the ground. There are a variety of methods used where the athlete runs a full or partial approach, executing the count step method of run-up and plant. The plant can be made into a folded towel or an extended piece of tape across the runway. However, for a more realistic effect, we suggest using a portable sliding box, commonly known as the "blow box." There are several commercial versions of this box, some of which are made of wood (Fig. 12-5).

FIGURE 12-5

By utilizing a "blow box" for drills, the vaulter can concentrate specifically on the run-up and the plant without compounding the problem by leaving the ground. It can also be used indoors without having to set up the vaulting pads.

When selecting a blow box, perhaps the best to use is a moderately heavy one (20-25 lbs). A weighted box will allow the vaulter and the coach to evaluate planting and directional force by noting how the pole bends and the rebounds of the sliding box. It is impossible to make these judgments using a lightweight box or towel.

Height of the Handhold

Probably the biggest advantage of the fiber glass vaulting pole lies in the ability of the vaulter to hold much higher than would be possible with the non-flexible pole. The common factors which determine the height are:

- general speed of the athlete;
- strength of the athlete;
- height of the athlete; and
- coordination and athletic ability

Everything being equal, the faster the athlete, the more force which is generated into the pole and, consequently, the faster the pole bends. This, of course, takes the "jolt" out of the plant. Strength not only contributes to the ability to run fast, but it is also important in changing horizontal velocity into a vertical force component at take-off. As in every track and field event, taller athletes have a definite advantage simply because there is less energy needed to move the center of mass in an upward direction. It is obvious that the taller the athlete, the higher he can grasp the pole.

Finally, coordination or simple athletic ability is necessary in utilizing a high pole grip. This innate characteristic dictates good timing and body control and will allow the vaulter to blend the run-up and plant transition.

By combining the above factors the vaulter is able to maximize the initial "shock" of a high pole plant.

The young vaulter may wish to determine a handhold to use with a short run-up when developing individual skill though part drills. To do this, he should stand facing the pit, place the pole tip on the ground, reaching up as high as possible with the top hand. Observe and mark the spot of this grip. Now, this marked spot becomes the grip point of the lower hand. The top hand position is 18"-24" above the low hand. This may vary slightly depending upon balance and comfort while carrying the pole.

After the vaulter has experience he can become much more specific as to an effective handhold. Remember, however, it is possible for a vaulter's hold to be too high to receive the maximum benefits (energy return) from the pole (its bending and lifting capabilities). The manufacturer's suggestions as to weight and hand hold should be followed. As a rule, poles are most effective when held approximately 9" from the top.

The Swing

The basic purpose of the swing action is simply to maintain momentum developed during the run-up, plant and take-off. The swing is actually dependent upon several very important items; first, it is initiated by a good energy-producing plant characterized by upper body penetration and with the center of weight positioned well back of the pole, and, secondly, by a high driving and "blocked" knee at the instant of take-off. The knee must move into a 90° angle, and be held at that angle, to provide impulse to the ground. This total action will provide a maximum split between that knee and the jumping take-off leg. It is important that the vaulter not allow this high knee to drop back down. The split must be maintained as long as possible.

FIGURE 12-6

Beginning the Swing with the wide split.

Prior to clearing the ground, the toe of the jumping foot should be pointing directly down toward the ground. This provides maximum extension of the jumping and swinging leg. From this plant extension, the leg should remain semi-extended throughout the remainder of the swing. The straighter the leg, the longer the lever and thus the more energy stored in the pole. The foot of the swing leg should move through a perfect circle. An ineffective, non-energy producing swing can easily be spotted by the foot moving through an "egg shaped" circle. It is important for the vaulter to maintain the swing until he gets into a complete vertical and upside down position. To do this, the athlete must not pull down with the top hand. The arm must stay extended throughout the entire swing. If this straight arm action occurs, the vaulter will automatically, with no conscious effort, go into the rock back body position. The swing of the bottom leg should continue its circular path until the moving foot catches and passes the plane of the still bent leading knee. (Fig. 12-7)

Only at this time should the pull and hip extension be initiated.

FIGURE 12-7

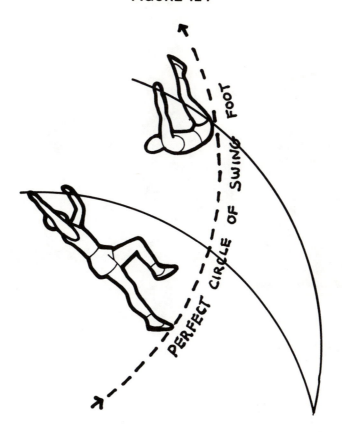

Pull and Turn

The pull should not begin until the pole is nearly straight. It is difficult to separate the action of the pull and the turn because the turn is actually initiated by the pull. As in all earlier sequences of the vault, the main objective is to keep the center of weight of the body from catching the pole until it straightens. The key is to deliver the muscular force of the pull at the exact instant the pole straightens. The vaulter seeks to shoot-up and away from the pole rather than simply fall away (Fig. 12-9).

At the time the pull-turn occurs, the vaulter now wants to be as close to the vertical alignment of the pole as possible. The pull, to be effective, must go directly through the hips. Equally important, the turn must occur beore the knees straighten out. If the athlete waits for the knees to extend before turning, his body weight will move ahead of the pole

FIGURE 12-8 **FIGURE 12-9** **FIGURE 12-10**

Pulling, turning and pushing *through the hips* with pole held close to the body.

and all power will be lost. The total body, i.e. legs, hips and shoulders, must turn at the same time. To be effective, the pulling action has to occur through the line of the pole. This can only occur if the hip and shoulder are in close contact with the pole.

I-II-III-IV Vault Technique Drills

by Ray Lewis

Once the young vaulter becomes knowledgeable about the various aspects of the vault, especially the run-up and the plant, he can begin to isolate the individual components of the vault with a 1-2-3-4 continuation drill series.

We would group the "whole skill" as: plant penetration; swing-rock back; turn; and pull hip extension turn. The drills are designed to develop each aspect individually, in order to blend them together for the total vault.

For all the following drills, the vaulter should select a "soft" pole, utilize a low hand hold and a short run-up approach.

Plant Penetration Drill

The idea here is for the vaulter, after a short run-up, to plant efficiently (see section on plant). During this maneuver, emphasis is placed upon exerting pressure with the bottom arm. He moves off the ground in a driving wide split position (Fig. 12-6). From this split position, the vaulter simply rides the pole through the pit with the feet pointing away from the runway. The drill objective is to isolate the drive-penetration from the ground.

The Swing Rock Back Drill

The second drill is a continuation of the plant penetration drill, but adds a new dimension—the swing-rock back. After the plant and chest penetration, the vaulter vigorously drives his lead leg up to his chest and the swinging trail leg moves to and is *held* at an upward vertical position (Fig. 12-8). Remaining in this position, the vaulter rides the pole through to the back of the pit. He will land on his back (in a back drop position) with the hips curled back and the toes pointing back toward the runway.

The Turn Drill

The turn drill is (1) initiated with a good plant penetration; (2) a swing-rock back; and (3) with a turn. The turn is accomplished during the swinging action when the knee has reached the chest. At this point, the swinging leg simply crosses (moves over and in front of) the leading leg. As the leg crosses, it immediately extends through the knee and the hip. Here again, the vaulter rides the pole through but now lands in a standing position facing the runway.

Pull Hip Extension, Turn Drill

During the sequence of (1), (2), and (3) as the vaulter crosses the swing leg, he now pulls vigorously with his arms and pushes (extends) his hips up the pole. He attempts to land standing in the pit facing the runway.

When it is possible for the vaulter to accomplish all these drills, he is ready to jump at the cross bar. When the total vault with the bar is attempted, the athlete should move to a heavier pole, raise the handhold somewhat and increase the runway distance. All of these should be done gradually as confidence, speed and technique improve.

As a vaulter's confidence, speed and technique improve, the vaulter should move to a heavier pole, raise the hand-hold somewhat and increase the runway distance.

WEEKLY WORKOUT
for
Vaulters

NAME: Kerby-Perkins   **DATE:** 1/20/82

1. **Easy jog**	21. **Workout of your choice**
2. **50 yds of high & fast leg**	22. **Warm-up** & check marks only
3. **70 yds. of stretch acceleration**	23. **Hurdle work**
4. **Sprint drills** (a) (b) (c)	**M** (1 to 1320)(Stretch)(2 full to 60) (20-40-20 with Poles)(16 H x 6) (14 A full)(stretching)
5. **Sprint belts**	
6. **Stadium stairs** a. Sprinting up b. Sprinting down c. Hopping up (1) single leg (2) double leg d. Hopping down (1) single leg (2) double leg	**T** (1 to 1320)(Stretch)(2 full to 60 (8 Blow Box x 15 min)(Full Vaults) (Trampoline)(Rope Work)
7. **Hill work** a. Protest (1) up hill (2) down hill b. Ann Morrison (1) up hill (2) down hill c. Americana (1) up hill (2) down hill	**W** (1 to 1320)(Stretch)(2 full to 60) (6a x6 for time)(6 c (1) x4) (6C 2 x4)(14A full)
8. **Runway drills**	**T** (Full Warm-Up)(Stretch) (8 counting, 9 Blow Box) (10-11 with C. Lewis)(15 to 3 miles)
9. **Planting drills**	
10. **Swing drills**	
11. **Pull-Push-turn drills**	
12. **Gymnastics** (a) tramp (b) high bar (c) rings	**F** (full warm-up) travel
13. **Rope** a. Pull-push turn b. Swing vaulting c. Stretch work	
14. **Weights** a. General (1) normal (2) circuit (3) power b. Special	**S** Compete at Pocatello
15. **Distance run**	
16. **Sets** a-40 b-50 c-60 d-70 e-80 f-100 g-110 h-165 i-180 j-220 k-330 l-352 m-440 n-500 o-550 p-600 q-660 r-880 s-1000	**S** Easy Run
17. **Drop downs** (same letters as above)	
18. **Gun starts** (same letters as above)	**Comments:**
19. **Continuous** relays (same letters as above)	
20. a. Meet with coach b. Film study c. Pictures	

KJELL ISAKSSON, SWEDEN

12-1

12-5   12-6   12-7

12-2   **12-3**   **12-4**

12-8   **12-9**   **12-10**

12-11   **12-12**   **12-13**   **12-14**

12-18   **12-19**

| 12-15 | 12-16 | 12-17 |

12-20

12-21   12-22   12-23

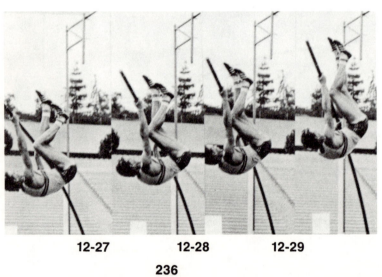

12-27   12-28   12-29

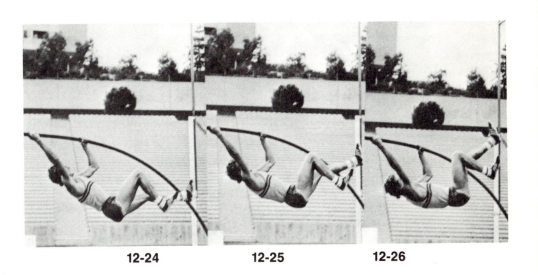

12-24   12-25   12-26

12-30   12-31   12-32   12-33   12-34   12-35

12-36   12-37   12-38

12-41   12-42   12-43

12-39   12-40

12-44   12-45

13

The Decathalon
by Bill Bakley

The decathlon is considered one of the most difficult events in track and field competition. It demands speed, agility, flexibility, strength and endurance. Training for such a varied event takes many hours, along with a well-defined plan on how to utilize the time available for the greatest benefit. The three key elements in the decathlon are:

● Desire and Dedication
● Time
● Planning

Desire and persistence are the key elements during the developmental phase because one does not become a star decathlete overnight. It takes time which should be pointed out to the beginning decathlete. It not only takes time but planning. Most great decathletes started out as skilled individual performers in one or two events and through planned development brought their weaker events up to the level of the more proficient ones.

So what is the Decathlon? The Decathlon consists of ten events contested over a two day period. These events are:

1st Day	2nd Day
100 meters	110 meters High Hurdles
Long Jump	Discus
Shot Put	Pole Vault
High Jump	Javelin
400 meters	1500 meters

241

Each of these events is performed in order with a half hour rest between events. Each competitor is given three attempts in the Long Jump, Shot Put, Discus and Javelin. In the High Jump and Pole Vault, three consecutive misses eliminates you from the competition, with the highest jump made counting in the scoring. The 100 meters, 400 meters and 1500 meters all have the three-false-start rule; on the third false start you are eliminated.

All times and distances are recorded with points being awarded for each. The points awarded are taken from the International Decathlon Scoring Tables. An abbreviated version of these tables appears later in this chapter. Totaling all ten event scores determines the winner of the competition. But one interesting fact remains, most decathletes do not compete against anyone but themselves. Competition is against the clock and tape measure. Each decathlete is trying to improve their score first before worrying about who wins.

Characteristics of a Decathlete

Size and weight are influencing factors in the decathlon. A man of average height (5'10"-6'2") and weight (175-190 lbs.) will be a prime candidate for a decathlete. Smaller men, like Jeff Bennett, and taller men, like Leonard Hedmark, are the exceptions who have been successful. Most champions have fallen into the average category.

Another characteristic trait of the decathlete is a sense of kinesthetic movement. Most athletes develop coordination and body mechanical awareness if they are in some sporting activity. With the wide range of movements and actions needed in the ten events, a good kinesthetic awareness is necessary. Even the most skilled kinesthetic performer can be reduced to an uncoordinated mass of humanity at the end of a decathlon. Be aware of the athlete with less than fully developed kinesthetic sense. He will need more attention in the skill events.

A decathlete should also be developed in these areas:

● **Strength:** A great deal of physical strength is required in the decathlon. Endurance, as well as brute strength is needed to master the running, jumping and throwing events. Good tendon strength and strength relative to body weight are also major elements. There is no way to strengthen a tendon, it is set, but it does help explosiveness. Tendon strength also has an influence in the prevention of injuries. Endurance, along with power, can be developed. A good balance between endurance, strength and power will benefit the athlete, so look for this key characteristic. High strength relative to body weight is a valued asset. Mass is needed for throwing, but is not needed for running or jumping. The problem of weight versus speed is one element that can be corrected with a proper integration of weights and running.

- **Desire:** This trait was mentioned earlier in the chapter as one of the key elements in a decathlete's makeup. Most successful athletes have a desire to win and compete, but a decathlete must also have a desire to perform the event itself. The event is too hard to spend the many hours it requires without loving it. Once the athlete is "hooked" on the event, a desire to become the "best" will develop without too much influence. A well-mapped plan will aid in developing the desire to be the best. The coach needs to channel desire into something that can aid the decathlete. Through encouragement, creation of goals and a plan of action, desire can be turned into a reality.

- **Dedication:** This characteristic was also mentioned earlier. Desire and dedication develop simultaneously during the training phase. An athlete who wants to win and loves to compete will spend the time developing the "perfect" technique or skill to become the best. The time spent on the field and in training will be quality time. Desire and dedication are mental attitudes that can be developed by the coach, and can produce very positive results in training and competition. We have found that desire and dedication remain high during practice when the skill events are broken down into small, integrated steps. Dedication can also be influenced with positive reinforcement. Encouragement during the developmental stage will produce quicker results, even for the seasoned performer. Through drilling and thousands of repetitions, skill and improvement take place. It is this improvement and success that encourage dedication and vice versa. If success is seen on a day-to-day basis, dedication will result. The decathlon is such a unique sport, even the beginner can find some event at which he is doing well. When that occurs, the opportunity is open for the coach to analyze the reason for the success and explain it to the athlete.

Planning

The success of the decathlete is dependent upon a well-mapped out plan. Desire, dedication and skills are only part of the entire training picture. A definite plan needs to be developed and implemented to provide direction and integration of physical and mental skills.

In any plan, time is the critical element in developing a skilled performer. The actual time a decathlete spends performing in competition is between 8 and 12 minutes. This performance time represents thousands of hours of preparation. Ten to twelve hours of training per day is common among world class decathletes. For the beginning decathlete, four to six hours is reasonable. The major portion of practice time is spent doing repetitive drills. In a meet, the major portion of time is spent resting and warming up for the next event. This presents a conflict in training. To rest a half hour between skills in practice is not an easy task. Certainly, practice is not a place to develop resting and the art of relaxation, but two-a-day workouts can help the athlete develop a plan to handle the break this type of scheduling creates.

When developing a yearly plan, three specific phases of training should be used; developmental, pre-competitive, and competitive, each phase lasting approximately four months. The gradual build-up throughout the program allows the decathlete to build conditioning, endurance, skill and strength before going to the next phase, thus preventing injuries, mental stress and skill mistakes from occurring.

Developmental Phase (4 Months)

June	July	August	September
-Run: 3-5 mi/da	-Run: 4-5 mi/da	-Run: 4-5 mi/da	-Run: 4-5 mi/da -hills 1 da/wk
-Wts: 4 da/wk -Str: 7 da/wk	-Wts: 4 da/wk -Str: 7 da/wk	-Wts: 4 da/wk -Str: 7 da/wk	-Wts: 4 da/wk -Str: 7 da/wk -Events: -Shot 1 da/wk -Dis 1 da/wk -Jav 1 da/wk

From the chart, one can see that the activities performed from June through August are similar, i.e., running, stretching and weight training.

June-August
Running: Mileage is important; 3-5 miles are run daily at moderate speed, creating a base to be drawn upon later.
Weights: See the training schedules provided.
Stretching: This is done everyday for at least ½ hour a day.

September
In September two changes occur; one day of hills is added per week and the throwing events start. The throwing should follow the pre-season schedule of the throwers including drills and skill development. (Refer to the specific event sections for all event work outlined in this chapter.)

Pre-Competitive Phase (4 Months)

The pre-competitive phase of training is a transition from base work to developing event skills and strength. At this point the decathlete is building up his endurance and strength for speed training. Each month builds on the previous one to create a progression providing the decathlete time and repetitiveness of skills to firmly place them in the nervous system. The activity that takes place should be watched by the coach so that the skills worked on will be done correctly and completely. This is the most critical part of the season. The decathlete will see a change in strength and event skills during this phase are all building for the next phase.

October	November	December	January
-Run: 3-5 mi/da -hills 1 da/wk -Wts: 4 da/wk -Str: 7 da/wk -Events: -shot 2 da/wk -disc 2 da/wk -jav 2 da/wk -H.H. 1 da/wk	-Run: 3-5 mi/da -hills 1 da/wk -Wts: 4 da/wk -Str: 7 da/wk -Events: -shot 2 da/wk -disc 2 da/wk -jav 2 da/wk -H.H. 1 da/wk -L.J. 1 da/wk -H.J. 1 da/wk	-Run: 3-5 mi/da -hills 1 da/wk -track 1 da/wk -Wts: 3 da/wk -Str: 7 da/wk -Events: -shot 2 da/wk -disc 2 da/wk -jav 2 da/wk -H.H. 2 da/wk -L.J. 2 da/wk -H.J. 2 da/wk -P.V. 1 da/wk	-Run: 3-5 mi/da -hills 1 da/wk -track 2 da/wk -Wts: 3 da/wk -Str: 7 da/wk -Events: -shot 1 da/wk -disc 1 da/wk -jav 1 da/wk -H.H. 2 da/wk -L.J. 2 da/wk -H.J. 2 da/wk -P.V. 2 da/wk

October:

Running: The same as the first phase, but the hills are increased in number and intensity.

Weights: They continue to build strength and endurance during this phase.

Stretching: Remains the same.

Events: Heavier implements are used in throws supplemented by an increased number of drills. The high hurdles begin, stressing running style and flexibility. Over the side and trail leg drills comprise the bulk of the workout.

November:

Running: The same with one day of track work added. This day consists of a large number of repeat intervals with short rest to start building the cardiovascular system.

Weights: An increase in weight with a decrease in sets.

Stretching: Remains the same, emphasis is concentrated on the legs.

Events: The throws receive more attention. The high hurdles will include going over the tops and developing better skills on negotiating the barriers. The jumps will start with drills and plyometrics to increase leg strength plus some early runway and run-up work will take place.

By December, the athlete should have learned most of the skills for the throws (shot, discus and javelin) and the high hurdles. December's workload will increase skill work in all areas along with the incorporation of more interval work to increase the speed factor.

December:
Running: Will intensify to include faster runs and more hill work. The track workouts will begin to develop some speed and endurance by using faster intervals with more rest between runs.
Weights: Now used three days per week; two days for endurance, one day for power.
Stretching: A basic stretching routine should have been established by now. Is now on those specific areas that seem tight.
Events: The throws will include work on the full throwing phase; but perfecting the techniques of the throws should continue. The high hurdles will implement full flights of hurdles, along with technique work on hurdles' clearance and running form. The jumps will incorporate box work, as well as skill work off the ground. Technique work will remain at a high level so full run-ups and runway work can be accomplished in January. The pole vault is added this month. The skills necessary to plant well are emphasized at this stage, i.e., pole carries, plants into a towel and plants into the box. Gymnastics are started this month.

January:
This is the transition month. More emphasis is placed on performance of the basic skills and implementing the events through a full range of motion with a high degree of speed and quickness.

Competitive Phase (4 Months)

Running: A tapering-off on hill work takes place with an increase in work on the track (2 days). This track work consists of one day of 400 meter training and one day of 1500 meter pace work.
Weights: Make a transition to 2 days of power and one day of endurance. Maximum strength lifting is emphasized.
Stretching: Remains the same.
Events: The throws should be close to proficiency. Full ring throwing and form correction will be paramount. The high hurdle form will show signs of being close to perfect, just waiting for the speed to be developed. Block work will start for both flat races and the high hurdles. The long jump work will stress balance on the board and on the landing. The high jump: work on being balanced at take off with much work on bar clearance. Pole vaulting takes place, with drills and gymnastics being paramount. Full vaulting will happen this month (1 day per week).

This last month brings us to the start of the outdoor season. The decathlete is ready for speed work and the little extras needed to bring about a skilled performance. As the athlete moves into the competitive season one thing must be emphasized, that the basic skill work should be complete and now the advanced skill work begins. Fast, hard running workouts will take place.

February	March	April	May

-Run: 3-4 mi/da
  -track 3 da/wk
  -road 3 da/wk
-Wts: 3 da/wk
-Str: 7 da/wk
-Events:
  -shot 1 da/wk
  -disc 1 da/wk
  -jav 1 da/wk
  -H.H. 2 da/wk
  -L.J. 2 da/wk
  -H.J. 2 da/wk
  -P.V. 2 da/wk
	-Run: 3-4 mi/da
	  -track 3 da/wk
	  -road 3 da/wk
	-Wts: 3 da/wk
	-Str: 7 da/wk
	-Events:
	  -weak 2 da/wk
	  -strong 2 da/wk
		-Run: 3-4 mi/da
		  -track 3 da/wk
		  -road 3 da/wk
		-Wts: 2-3 da/wk
		-Str: 7 da/wk
		-Events:
		  -weak 1 da/wk
		  -strong 3 da/wk
			-Run: 3-4 mi/da
			  -track 2 da/wk
			  -road 2 da/wk
			-Wts: 2 da/wk
			-Str: 7 da/wk
			-Events:
			  -weak 1 da/wk
			  -strong 2 da/wk

February:
Running: Increase to three days per week on the track. The extra day will be for fast, short, interval work. The rest between intervals will increase as the times and repetitions drop.
Weights: Remain the same.
Stretching: Remains the same.
Events: The throws will start to be de-emphasized to make time for the higher point events. The high hurdles will continue at the skill level of clearance. More starts will take place over hurdles. High Jump will be emphasized with landings and runway work being implemented. Pole Vault will emphasize full runway work, as well as jumping for maximum height.

March-April:
Running: More speed will be seen in the track workouts.
Weights: More power lifts will be used.
Stretch: Remain the same.
Events: The weak events will be de-emphasized with the stronger events developed to obtain the maximum performance level possible.

May:
As May arrives so do the major competitions. At this point all skills are at an optimum level, with emphasis being placed on speed and perfection of technique. Maximum strength is of prime importance with the

maintenance of the weak events and with improvements attempted in the strong one. All work and development are brought to bear this month. This is why the decathlete has been working, to compete on a high level. Maximum speed and execution are the primary elements.

Scoring Tables

The last part of this chapter contains an abbreviated decathlon scoring table. Each event is listed with a common English mark, the metric equivalent and the number of points awarded for that mark. In most decathlon meets, English marks will not be used, only metric. It would be worthwhile either to remember certain marks for the common English distances like 1.83 meters for 6'0 or invest in a metric conversion table. Either way, until the metric marks become a part of your track language, a conversion table is a valuable tool.

Decathlon Scoring Tables

(Abbreviated)

100 METERS

10.0 - 1072	11.0 - 804	12.0 - 580
10.1 - 1043	11.1 - 780	12.1 - 560
10.2 - 1014	11.2 - 756	12.2 - 540
10.3 - 986	11.3 - 733	12.3 - 520
10.4 - 959	11.4 - 710	12.4 - 501
10.5 - 932	11.5 - 687	12.5 - 482
10.6 - 905	11.6 - 665	12.6 - 463
10.7 - 879	11.7 - 643	12.7 - 444
10.8 - 853	11.8 - 622	12.8 - 426
10.9 - 828	11.9 - 601	12.9 - 408

LONG JUMP

17'0 - 5.18 - 415	19'9 - 6.02 - 608	22'6 - 6.86 - 791
17'3 - 5.26 - 434	20'0 - 6.09 - 624	22'9 - 6.93 - 806
17'6 - 5.33 - 541	20'3 - 6.17 - 642	23'0 - 7.01 - 822
17'9 - 5.41 - 470	20'6 - 6.25 - 660	23'3 - 7.08 - 836
18'0 - 5.48 - 486	20'9 - 6.32 - 675	23'6 - 7.16 - 853
18'3 - 5.56 - 505	21'0 - 6.40 - 693	23'9 - 7.24 - 869
18'6 - 5.64 - 523	21'3 - 6.47 - 708	24'0 - 7.31 - 883
18'9 - 5.71 - 539	21'6 - 6.55 - 725	24'3 - 7.39 - 899
19'0 - 5.79 - 557	21'9 - 6.63 - 742	24'6 - 7.47 - 915
19'3 - 5.86 - 573	22'0 - 6.70 - 757	24'9 - 7.54 - 929
19'6 - 5.94 - 591	22'3 - 6.78 - 774	25'0 - 7.62 - 945

SHOT PUT

32'0 - 9.75 - 441	37'6 - 11.43 - 561	43'0 - 13.10 - 671
32'6 - 9.90 - 453	38'0 - 11.58 - 571	43'6 - 13.26 - 682
33'0 - 10.06 - 464	38'6 - 11.73 - 581	44'0 - 13.41 - 691
33'6 - 10.20 - 475	39'0 - 11.88 - 591	44'6 - 13.55 - 700
34'0 - 10.36 - 487	39'6 - 12.04 - 602	45'0 - 13.55 - 700
34'6 - 10.50 - 497	40'0 - 12.19 - 612	45'6 - 13.87 - 720
35'0 - 10.67 - 509	40'6 - 12.34 - 622	46'0 - 14.01 - 729
35'6 - 10.81 - 519	41'0 - 12.49 - 632	46'6 - 14.17 - 739
36'0 - 10.97 - 530	41'6 - 12.65 - 642	47'0 - 14.31 - 747

HIGH JUMP

5'2 - 1.575 - 463	6'2 - 1.88 - 751	6'9 - 2.055 - 900
5'4 - 1.625 - 512	6'3 - 1.905 - 769	6'10 - 2.08 - 925
5'6 - 1.675 - 560	6'4 - 1.93 - 796	6'11 - 2.105 - 942
5'8 - 1.725 - 607	6'5 - 1.955 - 813	7'0 - 2.13 - 966
5'10 - 1.775 - 652	6'6 - 1.98 - 840	7'1 - 2.16 - 992
6'0 - 1.83 - 707	6'7 - 2.005 - 857	7'2 - 2.185 - 1009
6'1 - 1.855 - 725	6'8 - 2.03 - 882	7'3 - 2.24 - 1034

400 METERS

56.8 - 537	53.4 - 663	50.0 - 805
56.4 - 552	53.0 - 679	49.8 - 814
56.0 - 566	52.8 - 687	49.4 - 833
55.8 - 573	52.4 - 703	49.0 - 852
55.4 - 625	52.0 - 720	48.8 - 861
55.0 - 603	51.8 - 728	48.4 - 880
54.8 - 610	51.4 - 744	48.0 - 898
54.4 - 525	51.0 - 762	47.8 - 908
54.0 - 640	50.8 - 770	47.4 - 928
53.8 - 648	50.4 - 788	47.0 - 948

110 METER HIGH HURDLES

14.3 - 926	15.3 - 817	16.3 - 694
14.4 - 914	15.4 - 807	16.4 - 712
14.5 - 908	15.5 - 797	16.5 - 703
14.6 - 892	15.6 - 787	16.6 - 694
14.7 - 881	15.7 - 777	16.7 - 685
14.8 - 870	15.8 - 767	16.8 - 676
14.9 - 859	15.9 - 757	16.9 - 668
15.0 - 848	16.0 - 748	17.0 - 660
15.1 - 837	16.1 - 739	17.1 - 652
15.2 - 827	16.2 - 730	17.2 - 645

DISCUS

80 ' - 24.38 - 339	104' - 31.70 - 512	128' - 39.02 - 666
82 ' - 24.99 - 355	106' - 32.30 - 525	130' - 39.62 - 678
84 ' - 25.60 - 370	108' - 32.92 - 539	132' - 40.24 - 690
86 ' - 26.21 - 385	110' - 33.52 - 552	134' - 40.84 - 702
88 ' - 26.82 - 399	112' - 34.14 - 565	136' - 41.46 - 714
90 ' - 27.43 - 414	114' - 34.74 - 578	138' - 42.06 - 726
92 ' - 28.04 - 429	116' - 35.36 - 591	140' - 42.68 - 737
94 ' - 28.65 - 443	118' - 35.96 - 604	142' - 43.28 - 749
96 ' - 29.29 - 457	120' - 36.58 - 616	144' - 43.90 - 761
98 ' - 29.87 - 471	122' - 37.18 - 629	146' - 44.50 - 772
100' - 30.48 - 485	124' - 37.80 - 641	148' - 45.12 - 783
102' - 31.08 - 498	126' - 38.40 - 654	150' - 45.72 - 795

POLE VAULT

8'0 - 2.44 - 351	10'6 - 3.20 - 587	13'0 - 3.96 - 796
8'3 - 2.51 - 374	10'9 - 3.27 - 607	13'3 - 4.04 - 817
8'6 - 2.59 - 400	11'0 - 3.35 - 630	13'6 - 4.11 - 835
8'9 - 2.66 - 422	11'3 - 3.43 - 652	13'9 - 4.19 - 856
9'0 - 2.74 - 448	11'6 - 3.50 - 672	14'0 - 4.26 - 874
9'3 - 2.82 - 473	11'9 - 3.58 - 694	14'3 - 4.34 - 894
9'6 - 2.89 - 495	12'0 - 3.66 - 717	14'6 - 4.42 - 913
9'9 - 2.97 - 519	12'2 - 3.73 - 736	14'9 - 4.49 - 930
10'0 - 3.05 - 543	12'6 - 3.81 - 757	15'0 - 4.57 - 950
10'3 - 3.12 - 564	12'9 - 3.88 - 775	15'3 - 4.65 - 969

JAVELIN

80 ' - 24.38 - 227	130' - 39.62 - 485	180' - 54.86 - 697
85 ' - 25.91 - 256	135' - 41.14 - 508	185' - 56.38 - 716
90 ' - 27.43 - 284	140' - 42.68 - 530	190' - 57.92 - 735
95 ' - 28.95 - 311	145' - 44.20 - 552	195' - 59.44 - 754
100' - 30.48 - 338	150' - 45.72 - 574	200' - 60.69 - 773
105' - 32.00 - 364	155' - 47.24 - 595	205' - 62.48 - 791
110' - 33.52 - 389	160' - 48.78 - 616	210' - 64.00 - 809
115' - 35.06 - 414	165' - 50.30 - 637	215' - 65.54 - 828
120' - 36.58 - 438	170' - 51.82 - 657	220' - 67.06 - 845
125' - 38.10 - 462	175' - 53.34 - 677	225' - 68.58 - 863

1500 METERS

3:45 - 952	4:35 - 556	5:25 - 282
3:50 - 905	4:40 - 525	5:30 - 259
3:55 - 859	4:45 - 494	5:35 - 237
4:00 - 816	4:50 - 464	5:40 - 216
4:05 - 775	4:55 - 436	5:45 - 195
4:10 - 735	5:00 - 408	5:50 - 175
4:15 - 696	5:05 - 381	5:55 - 155
4:20 - 660	5:10 - 355	6:00 - 136
4:25 - 624	5:15 - 330	6:05 - 117
4:30 - 589	5:20 - 306	6:10 - 99

SAMPLE
MULTI-EVENT TRAINING SCHEDULE

NAME:

1. **Easy jogging**

2. **Warm-up drills:** a. High leg to 50 yds.;   b. Fast legs to 50 yds.;   c. 7x70 yds. acclerations; d. A-B-C's to 50 yds.;   e. Stretching

3. **Sprint belts**

4. **Stadium stairs**
   a. Sprinting up;   b. Sprinting down;
   c. Hopping up (1) Single leg, (2) Double leg;
   d. Hopping down (1) Single leg, (2) Double leg

5. **Hill work**
   a. Protext (1) up, (2) down
   b. Ann Morrison (1) up, (2) down
   c. Americana (1) up, (2) down

6. **Flat drills**
   a Bounding R-L-R-L for height 7 step approach
   b. R leg hops with 7 step approach
   c. L leg hops with 7 step approach
   d. Giant bounding (90 out rather than up)
   e. R-R-L-L-R-R-L-L etc.
   f. Hop step jump step jump etc.

7. **Running drills**
   a. Seven step approach 5 hop test (1) R leg, (2) L leg
   b. Seven step approach hop-step-step-step-jump
   c. 3 step (1) Long Jump, (2) High Jump, (3) Triple Jump
   d. 5 step (1) Long Jump, (2) High Jump (3) Triple Jump
   e. Full run up (1) Long Jump, (2) High Jump, (3) Triple Jump
   f. Pop-ups (1) 3 step, (2) seven step
   g. HHH
   h. Side hill running

12. **Drop downs** a. 40, b. 50, c. 60, d. 70, e. 80, f. 100, g. 110, h. 165, i. 180, j. 220, k. 330, l. 352 m. 440, n. 500, o. 550, p. 600, q. 880, r. 1000

13. **Gun starts** (same letters as above)

14. **Continuous relays** (same letters as above)

15. a. Meet with coach
    b. Films study
    c. Picture

16. **Workout of your choice**

17. **Warm-up and check marks only**

18. **Pool** a. swimming, b. intervals of shallow, c. intervals of deep

19. **Agility drills**
    a. Bench hopping
    b. Carioca running 5-10 x 40-50 yds.
    c. Lateral line drills
    d. Stretch turn leaps from a squatting position jump into the air making 360°
    e. Turn leaps over low hurdle
    f. Run intermediate hurdles

20. **Negative resistance**
    a. Overweight incline press
    b. Shot & discus incline

21. **Hungarian leg-power speed**
    a. Half jump squats
    b. Half jump squats
    c. Hopping backward on power leg
    d. Fast leg drills
    e. Standing long jumps
    f. Backward standing long jumps

8. **Boxes**
   a. 14-16' bounding R-L-R-L; 16-18 bounding R-L-R-L
   b. RR-LL
   c. Single leg through both legs
   d. HJ drills (1) Table jumping, (2) Ground to box to ground jumping, (3) Ground to low box jump
   e. Long jump drills (1) ground to box to ground jump, (2) ground to low box jump

9. **Weights**
   a. Special (1) clean & jerk, (2) single leg squats, (3) weighted vest, (4) lead leg drill
   b. Circuit
   c. Power strength (general)

10. **Running sets** a. 40, b. 50, c. 60, d. 70, e. 80, f. 100, g. 110, h. 165, i. 180, j. 220, k. 330, l. 352, m. 440, n. 500, o. 550, p. 600, q. 880, r. 1000

11. **Hurdles** (same letters as above)

22. **Throwing drills**
    a. scaling & South African
    b. Dry throwing
    c. overweight implements
    d. underweight implements
    e. standing throw
    f. full form throw

23. **See coach** a. film study   b. pictures

24. **Full warm-up & stretch out throwing**

25. **Pool** a. swimming   b. intervals-shallow c. intervals-deep

26. **Planting drills**

27. **Swing drills**

28. **Pull-Push-turn drills**

29. **Gymnastics** a. tramp   b. high bar   c. rings

30. **Rope**
    a. Pull-push turn
    b. Swing vaulting
    c. Stretch work

SELECTED REFERENCES

Bergen, Scoles. *Weight Training: A Systematic Approach.* Ames, Iowa: Iowa State University, 1981.

Ballard and Knuth. *Triple Jump Encyclopedia.* Pasadena, Ca.: The Athletic Press, 1977.

Bunn, John. *Scientific Principles of Coaching.* Englewood Cliffs, N.J.: Prentice Hall, 1955.

Christensen, E.H. "New Research in Results from Interval Work in the Field of Sports Medicine." *Der Sportarzt Vereinigt Mit Sport-Medizin,* June 1961.

Councilman, James. "conditioning of Competitive Swimmers." *Proceedings of the Sixth Medical Association National Conference on the Medical Aspects of Sport.* Bloomington, Ind.: American Medical Association, 1965.

Daniels, Jack; Felts, Robert; and Sheehan, George. *Conditioning for Distance Running.* New York: John Wiley and Sons, 1978.

Doherty, Kenneth. "Omnibook." *Track and Field News,* 1971.

Dyatchkov, Vladimir. "How the Russian High Jumpers Succeeded at Rome." *Track Technique,* June 1961.

Dyson, Geoffrey. *The Mechanics of Athletics.* London: Homes and Meier Publisher, 1974.

Ecker, Tom. "Track and Field—Technique through Dynamics." *Track and Field News,* 1971.

Ecker, Tom. "Track and Field Techniques through Dynamics." *Track and Field News,* 1976.

Edsrom L., and Ekblom, B. *Differences in Sizes of Red and White Muscle Fibers in Vastus Lateralis of Quadriceps Femoris of Normal Individuals and Athletes.* Scand. J. Clinical Investigation 30: pp. 175-181, 1972.

Falk, Bill. *Taking the Mystery Out of Fiberglass Pole Vaulting.* Providence, R.I.: The M-F Athletic Company Inc., 1972.

Frankl, R., and Caalay, L. "Effects of Regular Muscular Activity on Adreno-Cortical Function of Rats." *The Journal of Sports Medicine and Physical Education, II:* No. 4 (Dec. 1962).

Gambetta, Vern. "Plyometric Training." *California Track News,* Jan.-Feb. 1977.

Ganslen, Richard. "Aerodynamics and Mechanical Forces in Discus Flight." *The Athletic Journal,* April 1964.

Gerschler, Woldemar. "Training of Middle and Long Distance Runners." *Track Technique, XVIII,* Sept. 1964.

Guyton, Arthur. *Textbook of Medical Physiology.* Philadelphia and London: The W.B. Saunders Co., 1968.

Hay, James G. "The Hay Technique." *Track and Field Quarterly,* Fall 1977.

Hay, James G. *The Biomechanics of Sports Techniques.* Englewood Cliffs, N.J.: Prentice Hall 1978.

Heger, W. "Is the Rotation Technique Better?" *Track Technique,* December 1974.

Henry, Franklin. "Research on Sprint Running." *The Athletic Journal,* February 1952.

Jcoby, Ed. *Get Set.* Boise, Id.: Boise State University Printing and Graphics, 1980.

Jacoby, Ed. "Physiological Implications of Interval Training." *National Track Coaches Quarterly Review,* March 1969.

Kochel, Guy. *Practical Coaching Techniques for the Pole Vault.* Ames, Ia.: Championship Books, 1981.

Koltai, J. "Evaluating the Discus Style of Shot Put." *Track Technique,* 1975.

Lydiard, Arthur. "Running Training Schedules." *Track and Field News,* 1965.

Morehouse, L., and Miller, A. *Physioloy of Exercise.* St. Louis, Mo.: C.V. Mosby, 1976.

Prokop, Ludwig. "Arenals and Sport." *The Journal of Sports Medicine and Physical Fitness, III:* No. 2-3, June-Sept., 1963.

Raimondo, Vincent D. "Function of the Adrenal Cortex." *The Adrenal Cortex.* Paul B. Hoeber, Inc.; Medical Division of Harper and Brothers, 1961.

Robison, Jensen, James, and Hierschi. *Modern Techniques of Track and Field.* Philadelphia: Lea and Febiger, 1974.

Rompotti, Kalevi. "The Blood Test as a Guide to Training." *Track Technique,* September 1960.

Roskamm, H.; Reindell, H.; and Keul, J. *About the Question Regarding the Effects of Phases in Interval Training.* Der Sportazt Vereingt Mit Sportmediz. Indianapolis, In.: Phi Epsilon Kappa Physical Educator, June 1961.

Ross, Wilbur. *The Stress of Life.* New York: McGraw-Hill, 1965.

Spindler, John. "The Physiological Basis of Interval Training." *United States Track Coaches Quarterly Review,* December 1966.

Tansley, John. *The Flop Book.* Santa Monica, Cal.: Peterson Lithographic Corp., 1980.

Tuttle, W., and Schottelus, Byron. *A Textbook of Physiology.* St. Louis, Mo.: C.V. Mosby, 1969.

Veroshanskly, Yuiry. *Legkaya Athletics.* Soviet Sports Review, Translated by Michael Yessis,

California State University at Fullerton, 1960.
Wilt, Fred. "Stress Training." *Track Technique,* Sept., 1960.
Wilt, Fred. "How They Train." *Track and Field News,* 1968.
Wilt, Fred. "Plyometrics, What It Is and How It Works." *Athletic Journal*, Vol. 66, May 1975.